Intake Specialists

The Unsung Heroes of® Law Firms Worldwide™

Volume I – 2nd Edition

Chris Mullins, **Intake Academy**™ LLC
Harlan Schillinger, **Network Affiliates, Inc.**

Design / Editorial: Deb Morrison

Chris Mullins Empire™
© 2015 Mullins Media Group™ LLC
All rights reserved

ISBN: 978-0-9963600-0-5
Volume I – 2nd Edition

Reproduction or translation of any part of this work without express permission of the publisher is unlawful. Requests for permission or further information should be addressed to the publisher at:

Mullins Media Group™ LLC
507 Greenfield Road
Peterborough, New Hampshire 03458
United States

New Hampshire Office:
(603) 924-1640
Fax: (603) 924-5770

Business Office:
beth@mullinsmediagroup.com
chris@mullinsmediagroup.com

www.MullinsMediaGroup.com

Additional Resources

➤ Opt-in at www.GreatBottomLine.com to get Chris Mullins' famous FREE Monday Morning Email Stimulator™

➤ Opt-in at www.IntakeAcademy.com to get your FREE Video Email Coaching Series with Chris Mullins

Why Read This Book?

Mullins Media Group™ LLC publishes easy-to-read, how-to sales and business books for all types of businesses — whether butcher, baker or candlestick maker. We publish books that focus on the team, the unsung heroes of your business, the individuals who are communicating with your prospects, clients and patients by telephone. These people are also known as the first impressions director, the front desk, the receptionist, the sales team, customer service and the call center.

Our goal is to shine a bright light on the team so that the business owner, CEO, COO — from the top down — is reminded how critical these individuals are to their bottom line. Our books are an important, necessary tool and guide to support all business owners worldwide. Leaders who master our books will be able to endure all the challenges they face, so that they can continue to coach, support and motivate their very own team to want them to follow them into any battle — no matter what.

Disclaimer

This book is designed to provide information about the subject matter covered. It is sold with the understanding that the publisher and authors are not hereby engaged in rendering legal, psychological or other professional services. If expert assistance is required, the services of a competent professional should be sought. We are available for consultation on a professional basis.

Every effort has been made to make this book as complete and accurate as possible. However, there may be mistakes both typographical and in content. Therefore, this text should be used only as a general guide.

The purpose of this book is to educate and entertain. The authors and publisher shall have neither liability nor responsibility to any person or entity with respect to any loss or damage caused or alleged to be caused directly or indirectly by the information contained herein.

INTAKE™ ACADEMY LLC
www.IntakeAcademy.com
A Division of Mullins Media Group™ LLC

Contents

About Harlan Schillinger, page 6
Foreword by Harlan Schillinger, page 7
About Chris Mullins, page 34

Interview
Chris Mullins Interviews Harlan Schillinger 9
Harlan Schillinger
    Never Send a Prospect to a Lawyer 26
    Arming Your Ambassador of First Impressions 27
    Answering the Call! 28
    Four Tracking Tactics You Must Do 29
    Harlan Schillinger Testimonials 30

Chapter 1
Five Intake Specialist Heroes: Real Lives, Real Stories 37
    Chris Mullins Interviews Intake Hero #1 38
    Chris Mullins Interviews Intake Hero #2 46
    Chris Mullins Interviews Intake Hero #3 54
    Chris Mullins Interviews Intake Hero #4 60
    Chris Mullins Interviews Intake Hero #5 68

Chapter 2
Intake Academy Students Share Their WILs 77

Chapter 3
Chris Mullins 93
    The Evolution Infrastructure of the Receptionist 94
    Your Business' Most Important Tool 112
    Scripts and How to Use Them 124
    Where Does the Receptionist and Intake Specialist
        Come In? 134

Chapter 4
FAQs With Chris Mullins 147

Chapter 5
Intake Academy Newsletter 163

Quiet Rooms for Law Firms™ 174

Intake Academy Services 176

We're Growing!
And We're Looking for Phone Coaches and Trainers 178

Join the Community of Intake Specialists Worldwide

Do you know an intake specialist, receptionist, first impressions director that you would like to nominate for our next book, *Intake Specialists: The Unsung Heroes of Law Firms Worldwide, Volume 2*? If so, email beth@intakeacademy.com and put NOMINATE in the subject line. Make sure to include the full name, email, business name and the phone number of the person you're nominating. Share with us why you're nominating them and our office will contact you for the next step. Thank you for supporting the world of intake specialists.

Do you have a recommendation for a book or books that we should consider publishing for other areas and individuals of the law firms? We would love to hear your idea. Email beth@intakeacademy.com and put BOOK IDEA in the subject line.

Attorneys Only
Get Your FREE Mystery Call and Conversion Debrief

Go to **www.IntakeAcademy.com** and on the first page just click on *Sign Up for Free Mystery Call*. As you go through the sign-up, don't forget to schedule your **Attorney-Only** and **Chris Mullins Mystery Call Conversion Debrief**.

Heroes Stop What They're Doing to Help Others

The five heroes we celebrate in this book will be part of a very special raffle. Intake Academy will put each name into the proverbial "hat" and once the book is published, a name will be selected. This person will have $500 donated by the Intake Academy in their name to their favorite charity. *Congratulations to all our heroes and thank you for what you do — every day!*

The Trial Lawyer, A Magazine for Trial Lawyers & a Voice for Justice

The Trial Lawyer magazine (www.thetriallawyermagazine.com) provides progressive and educational news, information, and articles relevant to the trial lawyer profession. Our mission is to inform and inspire trial attorneys who represent injured individuals in civil cases or defend the accused as guaranteed under the United States Constitution.

The Trial Lawyer strives to create innovative forum for understanding current trends and emerging opportunities for the civil plaintiff or criminal defense trial bar. Through passionate voices and provocative viewpoints, The Trial Lawyer encourages the generation and sharing of ideas through open dialogue among the finest trial lawyers in America.

Make sure to read Chris Mullins' article published in the 2014 Summer issue (on page 12) entitled "A Four-Step Lead Conversion System to Generate More Clients."

Resource: Legal Intake Specialists Association™ (LISA). To learn more, email beth@intakeacademy.com or call (603) 924-1640 and ask for more information about LISA.

About Harlan Schillinger
Old School Ethics; Aggressive Representation

"I start my days and base my relationships trying to establish a fair and equal exchange of value," says Harlan Schillinger. Harlan is a 38-year veteran of the advertising industry who joined Network Affiliates (www.netaff.com) in 1985 to lead its marketing efforts. Network Affiliates currently represents over 88 clients in over 96 markets. It is considered the pioneer and premier advertising agency for legal advertising and marketing.

Prior to joining Network Affiliates, Harlan was vice president and one of the founding partners of Madison, Muyskens & Jones in Lakeville, Connecticut. Along with his partners, Harlan founded the first syndication firm for retailers using television commercials throughout the United States.

Knowing your business and searching out opportunities for clients is one of his strongest agendas. Throughout the year, Harlan attends conventions and speaks at attorney meetings and participates in prominent roundtable forums throughout the country as a speaker, moderator and contributor in order to help his clients stay on top of the legal field. He is deeply involved with the National Trial Lawyers Summit, 360 Advocate and PILMMA.

"Creating opportunities and increasing market share for my clients is my No. 1 priority in this tough economy," he says.

Harlan is an avid motorcycle enthusiast who enjoys being a member of the most unique and prestigious custom motorcycle club in the world — the Hamsters USA. His passions are building and riding custom motorcycles and trying to playing golf. Harlan also sits on the Board of the Children's Care Hospital and School in South Dakota (www.cchs.org), a hospital dedicated to helping special needs children.

Driven by passion, he is a real lover of life. *"If you're not rubbin, you're not racin'."* – DE, Jr. (Thanks, Dale Jr., for letting me use your line.)

Specialties: Aggressive, creative, polished and successful advertising, marketing and public relations!

Foreword

The real hero of the law firm has always been sitting, patiently, at the front desk. Although I've worked at the country's pioneering legal marketing and advertising agency for over 29 years, this fact didn't really sink in until the day I met this person eye to eye. I walked into my client's law office, and there she greeted me with a genuine smile and kind words that I'll never forget. It was like the whole law firm had hugged me. And at that moment this heroine was forever coined the Ambassador of First Impressions™. Today I use that term whenever I'm talking to lawyers about the absolutely critical component of intake.

In fact, I'm so passionate about intake and conversion that I'll tell you here and now that it's one of if not the most important elements of legal marketing. You can spend hundreds, thousands, even millions of dollars on the snazziest television campaigns in town, but if you can't convert a call to a case with a solid intake plan and personnel, you're toast. Burnt, finished, done — and gone!

Let me reiterate: The people you have answering your firm's phones are your lifeline. They set the tone for how your practice is known by the public, and they alone can transform a lead into a lucrative case. And for that, these intake specialists should be validated. Supported, educated and thanked.

On that day when that big, bright grin spoke to me, she was thrilled with her new title — Ambassador of First Impressions™. When I mentioned the term in front of her boss — you know, the big lawyer with his name on the building — her beam magnified. She literally started to glow. Why? Because this was the first day that someone had truly authenticated the value of her role at the law firm. She got it and the boss got it!

This book is all about the importance of intake. But really, it's a story about your people. You'll learn about intake's ROI, but you'll also start to measure the worth of those who sit next to you every day. May you take away from *The Unsung Heroes of Law Firms Worldwide* the tools you need to boost your business, but also the moral in making your real heroes proud to answer the call of duty. Remember, intake is everything! Enjoy.

Chris Mullins & Harlan Schillinger
Interview

Chris Mullins Interviews Harlan Schillinger of Network Affiliates

Mullins: We're going to talk about our wonderful new book, *Intake Specialists: The Unsung Heroes of Law Firms Worldwide*. Harlan, why don't you begin by introducing yourself and say a little bit about what it is that you do?

Schillinger: First of all, I really appreciate having the opportunity to do this with you. I'm a veteran of the legal community and I currently work with 96 markets and about 88 firms around the country, so I have an absolutely great appreciation for what you do.

As I've always said to you since the day I met you, I need you more than you need me. The reason being is that my ad agency generates thousands of calls a month right along with what we do in a year. I am deeply concerned about how those calls are answered and how they are converted into quality business. I believe that you have a key to an unlocked door that is quite obvious and people should absolutely recognize it and that's why we're on this phone call.

Mullins: The reason why the Intake Academy is talking with you is because, quite honestly for me, I could feel your passion as a sincere individual, a person and a professional in the law industry. That's the reason I asked if you would be interested in doing this.

Schillinger: Oh, it's gotten to be an absolute necessity. Quite frankly, intake in a law firm, although we all want to feel that it's unique and we all want to feel how special it is, is special because you do have people who need help and you have to weed through all of that to find the sincere nuggets of people who really have honest and legitimate situations. Whether you call a credit card company or you call your cable company because your service is not working and who you speak to... quite frankly, it's called customer service.

> ...people who need help and you have to weed through all of that to find the sincere nuggets of people who really have honest and legitimate situations.

If you were to ask a lawyer what he/she does for a living, my first answer is "we go after the bad guys." That's what my clients do for a living. Yes, they're lawyers. People don't understand what lawyers do, but when somebody is hurt, somebody is injured or somebody simply has a question, they pick up the telephone. How that call is answered will determine the rest of it. That's why I'm so passionate about it. Passionate out of necessity.

Mullins: I hear that from you so I'm going to ask. I want to dig in a little bit more. We've worked with thousands of companies and I personally have been doing this for 25 years, mostly with law firms, but also in other businesses. And it's few and far between to find leaders in an industry like yours who are so passionate, but also obsessed with how people answer the phones. Try to help people to understand the value of that.

Schillinger: Well, let me give you the nuts and bolts of this in the simplest way I can. Last year, my clients spent well over $30 million combined in advertising. Let's take one client in any market that's spending any amount of money, but hypothetically, let's say he's spending half-a-million dollars in the course of a year. Half-a-million dollars on television in a medium-sized market is a ton of money. They're spending all of this money and time to get a return, and what they're counting is what cases they've got at the end of the day.

I'm not accounting for how they got those cases or, more importantly, how they didn't get those cases. It takes a huge amount of money to get the phone to ring, and they spend a lot less effort to weed through what is coming at them or take the time to understand who is calling or cultivate that. They need to think more about that, account for more of what is coming at them, listen more carefully to the clients and then two things could happen.

> **Attorneys are spending all of this money and time to get a return, and what they are counting is what cases they've got at the end of the day.**

Number one, they'd get a far better yield to the same amount of dollars. Second, they would develop future business on how you treat people, because at the end of the day, personal injury... and you can take this to the bank, people don't know if they got a good settlement or a bad settlement. They know how they were treated. And that treatment begins with, "Hello, I'm the law firm of blah, blah, blah. May I help you?" From that moment on will determine everything and that's why I'm passionate about it.

Mullins: Something that you say often... actually, every time, quite frankly, I bump into you or when I talk to you on the phone, you say the same thing over and over again — that you need the Intake Academy more than the Intake Academy needs you. Why do you say that?

Schillinger: I am desperate to get my clients to understand intake and conversion. They simply don't get it because they don't understand accountability. Quite frankly, I am emphatic that I need you more than you need me because we do our jobs very well. We make the phone ring and my clients make a ton of money but they're always wanting to bring in more cases.

And the only sensible way to bring more cases or to make the best of what they spend is to understand this intake process better. They're terrible at it. That is why I need you more than you need me, because you have the keys to the door. You understand the process. You know how to teach people with conversion and how to answer the telephone much more effectively. I

> It takes a huge amount of money to get the phone to ring and they spend a lot less effort to weed through what is coming at them or take the time to understand who is calling or cultivate that.

think I do but you are more of an expert. You're more articulate. You have a solid plan on how to train and teach people how to change their ways and get a far better yield for the same money.

Mullins: I'm going to ask you another question. Here you are, a legal marketing expert, an advertising agency and you have all of these clients. Your clients are spending money with you so you can do what you do well, which is get the phone to ring. Well, if your clients just want to keep spending more and more money with you to get the phone to ring more, from their point of view, why are you so focused on slowing them down and putting the brakes on the part of, "Wait a minute, it's not about spending more money, it's about converting what you have"?

Schillinger: They are not making the best of what's coming in the door. They are seeing approximately 20% of the phone calls that they receive turn into cases. They want 30% to turn into cases, 40%, 50%, and the fact of the matter is, the cases are in front of them. They have to recognize what a good case or a bad case is and slow the process down so that they can achieve more quality, because quantity is not necessarily the answer. If they were to spend more money to generate calls, their percentage of conversion would not change. It would cost them significantly more to gather the case by spending more money to get more leads.

> They are not making the best of what's coming in the door. They are getting approximately 20% of the phone calls that they receive turn into cases.

The key is answering the leads effectively and getting better yield, which would bring the cost of case acquisition down. And that is the most legitimate, honorable and profitable way for a law firm to increase their business.

Mullins: It's also your truth, isn't it?

Schillinger: What do you mean by that?

Mullins: You're always saying that you're not trying to sell. You're speaking the truth that this is what your clients need to focus on to be able to do what they want to do, which is to convert more and help more people.

Schillinger: Absolutely, Chris. This is not about you. It is not about your Intake Academy. This is about my clients doing better. You happen to have the keys to the candy store because you are experts at what you do. I approached you because I needed your help in delivering that message to my clients. There are a number of people who do this. There are very few people in the world who understand it and do it as well as you.

So when I look for somebody to deliver a message, I look around and try to find the best person and the best people who are out there. I know there are a very few and select people who get it, and you have 25 years of teaching people how to change habits, which is a very difficult thing. But there isn't any question. This is not as much about you as it is my client. My clients have to recognize that there is a problem and an opportunity. I'm asking you because you're so articulate at delivering the message.

> The key is answering the leads effectively and getting better yield which would bring the cost of case acquisition down.

Mullins: You know, one of the biggest things that I worry about is I really do have concern for the individuals: the intake specialist, the receptionist, the front desk, the call center agents, folks on the front line who are actually taking these phone calls every day all day long.

Our In-House Team of Certified Coaches monitor and listen to real prospective client phone calls that agencies like yours supply to your clients over and over again, every single month. We hear those real calls and the stories and the emotional tragedy. What the intake specialist is hearing and listening to all day long, one call after another, is absolutely shocking.

And that's why we're doing this book. That's why we think they are heroes and we want them to realize it. But we also want the attorneys, the senior level of executives, the managing partners from the top down to really embrace their team first and focus on them.

One of the things that you shared with me on the phone was about… tell me if I got this right, the ambassador of first impression. And you told me a story that when you go and visit clients, one of the first things you do involves a business card. Do you want to share that a little bit with everybody?

Schillinger: Yes, because I feel very strongly about this. But I'm going to answer with an analogy. You know, when you're going to battle and all the generals are standing around their desks and they have their maps out and they have the greatest intentions to outline their assault and how they're going to win this battle. The thing that is most interesting is you can have the brightest generals in the world and have the greatest plan, but the people who are really the heroes of the battle are the soldiers.

If you don't have the right soldiers in place and support the soldiers, feel passionate about them and recognize and respect them, because these are the people at the very beginning of the battle, on the battlefield, representing you, then you're not going to win the war. All the generals on the planet can come up with the greatest orders, but they have to be executed, and at the end of the day, you win wars by having boots on the ground.

> The thing that is most interesting is you can have the brightest generals in the world and have the greatest plan, but the people who are really the heroes of the battle are the soldiers.

So I feel very passionate about this and I discover it when I walk into a client or a prospect's office. I know who the very first person that I'm going to say hello to is — the receptionist — the very first person that is going to receive the very first telephone call.

I have so much respect for that situation that when I walk in, I want them to know that. I hand them a business card with a new title that mirrors the standard business card but the title says, "I am your ambassador of first impressions." What that specifically recognizes is how important they are and gives them the understanding that "I really think you're important and you are." What's more important than the very first word you say to somebody you've just met? I'm basically empowering them and empowerment is a very strong and motivating tool.

Mullins: I think that's awesome and that's why we were attracted to you. That's why we've all aligned together here today to talk about this book because you feel the same things. I used to do the job of the intake specialist for newspapers, the front desk and call centers.

I know what it's like to deal with it. But the calls that these folks are handling, the stories... You've got some people on a phone call that are talking about how their family died and they're being so graphic and so detailed and the folks that are handling the calls, they're amazing with what they're doing.

I'm happy to hear that you actually go out of your way to create a business card, stop by the front desk or intake and actually pass it out to them. That's amazing.

Schillinger: Well, it's truthful and what I'm doing is I'm respecting them just as I would anybody else. You know, intake is an interesting thing whether it's in a law firm or whether it's a car wash. Intake means that you're intaking information into your mind to respond to people. When you first meet somebody, you are an intake specialist in your own way. We're honing in on law firms because we recognize that it's our business, and our mission in life is to help our clients do better. And by doing better, it's practicing business in an ethical and passionate way.

It really comes down to if you take a look at any oath that a lawyer ever finds before getting his license. Before taking on a client, by the way, I go to the Internet and I ask my client or prospect to read the contract that he made with the state that he is licensed in. And there's some very specific language in that. He promises to uphold the law, to treat his clients with dignity, to work vigorously for that, to do everything in his power to ethically represent them. It's amazing how many lawyers sign that. You have to sign the oath to get your license, but they sign it and then over the years, they kind of forget about that.

Mullins: Right.

Schillinger: What we're doing is asking those soldiers, those people on the front line, to do is to represent that oath to the best of their ability. And that's where the compassion, that's where the listening and that's where the difficulty of their job comes in. This is not a business. This is a profession. It's run like a business because bills have to be paid. You have certain accruements that you have to follow through on. But we'll never get away from the fact that a human being is calling you for help, and how you respond to that will define your character.

Mullins: Absolutely. What we feel is really important is focusing on your team first. If you, the business owner, the managing partner, the senior level executive, focus on your internal customer service, your team of front line individuals, and you give them everything that they need to run your business, they're like mini business owners. It's like they have a franchise of your business. And if you give them everything that they need — recognition, motivation, reward, ongoing coaching and training and attention and all the tools that they need — if you do that for them, then it's going to be there for all of your clients and all of your prospective clients. The other thing that it really helps is retention. It's not just retention for clients, but it's also retention of team members.

In the concept of intake, the intake world, the intake universe/front desk/receptionist, those particular kinds of positions tend to be like a revolving door. One reason is that they tend to be, believe it or not, the easiest jobs to get because of the way business owners and law firms are hiring for them. They want people who can sit in the chair who can show that their resume says they stayed at a business for a decent period of time and they check some references. The applicant says they love to talk on the phone. They sound like they can talk on the phone.

> But we'll never get away from the fact that a human being is calling you for help, and how you respond to that will define your character.

You know they're just getting people in the chairs. There really is not a lot of focused screening and processing going on when you're looking for an intake specialist. So anybody can get that job and anybody is going to say, "Oh, I can do that. I can talk on the phone…"

Schillinger: Well, Chris, with all due respect, one of the reasons it's an easier job to find for the employee is because so many people just left or somebody was just released from there and so the void needs to be filled.

And you're 100% correct. The owners of firms put the least amount of resources and the least amount of recognition into probably the most important job in the office. The reason that I think it's an easy job to get is because employers are so desperate to fill it they don't realize why it's empty in the first place or why the void

> The other thing that it really helps is retention. It's not just retention for clients, but it's also retention of team members.

is there in the first place. So, with all due respect, it's the hardest job in the office to find and the least recognized. When you called me and said, "Hey, listen. What do you think about this?" without telling me you're writing a book or asking for my help, I said, "My God, I think you really hit the nail on the head. You know, let's talk about the soldiers. Let's talk about the people who go to work every day." When you dissect it and take a good look at it, they *are* the unsung heroes.

Mullins: Harlan, let me ask you this. Do you think that the position lends itself to that kind of burnout? Obviously we've talked about the recognition, some of the lack of recognition in the law firm, but also just the nature of the jobs. So, here this person is taking call after call and they're hearing tragic stories, these are tragic incidents.

Like you said, part of their job is having to sift through all of these different inquiry calls. Some of them are not legitimate, some of them are people who are looking for a frivolous law suit or something like that, but obviously there are people out there who genuinely need help and they have a case. Do you think that the position, having to go through that, just burns people out?

Schillinger: No. I do not think that the clients and the person dumping on the intake specialist burns the intake specialist out. I think that they love the position. It's empowering. They like helping people. I specifically have put thought into this and I can tell you, in my opinion, what I think burns the intake specialist out is the lack of recognition, it's the lack of system, it's the lack of accountability from the intake specialist point forward.

It's taking care of this special person who is very much in need of help and handing it over to a lawyer who is too busy to call them back or has to wait three days to acknowledge that this person is in a hospital. Or this person was injured because the systems aren't in place and the empathy isn't in place. I believe that the lack of systems and the lack of support is what significantly burns them out quicker.

Mullins: I have to ask a question. I know this is not what we're talking about, but I'm just banging my head against the wall right now. I'm thinking about our clients and I think where this is coming from is as someone who's been coaching and training businesses, not just law firms, for 25 years doing the same kind of program.

I am shocked at how much the law firms have no systems in place and no processes for intake. I'm talking about law firms like you're talking about now. I'm not going to mention any names but some are large celebrity law firms that are doing very well. There are about a thousand employees, for example, for some of them and they are doing

Interview With Harlan Schillinger   17

all the latest and greatest in marketing. They're doing all the right stuff. They're spending the money on it. They're doing all of that.

Schillinger: And they're usually pretty good lawyers.

Mullins: Exactly right, and they're good people, too. When you have that kind of make-up, I would think that when I go in they're going to have everything game-on with regards to intake. I tell you, when I'm looking at it, there's nothing there.

Schillinger: Well, if you would like my unvarnished opinion on that, I am more than happy to share.

Mullins: Go right ahead.

Schillinger: My unvarnished opinion is that they're making too much money. And this is kind of funny. I think you said this to me and I just grabbed hold of it. These guys think that they're very smart because they're making a lot of money. But the truth of the matter is they could do so much better if they had better systems in place. When you're in law school, they give you business courses for about one quarter of a semester.

Mullins: Right.

Schillinger: And when you're in medical school, they don't focus on the business aspect of managing management at all. You're absolutely correct. I think what's going on is that you could have the worst systems in the world because this is the only business that I know of where there is no ceiling. There is no tap on how much you can win in a law suit or win for your client. They've got so much coming at them and it's very difficult to tell a financially successful law firm that it could do so much better. And what's going on right now is because of competition, because of the way things are in the world, things are tightening up.

The law firms that didn't have to pay attention to any of this before have to pay attention to it now because of the competition, so they're running scared and it's amazing. You are absolutely right on this, Chris, about how could they operate in this manner. I'm appalled and I'm in, like I said, 96 markets. I'm appalled at the lack of software and the lack of tools that we have attributed to this department. You know, we're in a technologically savvy society.

Mullins: I know.

Schillinger: It doesn't take a rocket scientist to buy a piece of software, whether it's Salesforce or something like that, so you can track your leads, track your on-leads, track your non-leads. Since this is a free-flowing conversation, I'll give you an example. I was in New Orleans, in a meeting with 23 lawyers, and I was the only advertising affiliate invited. I was told I was invited because I share unselfishly my experiences and options. There were five people in the room, five people who were my clients. The rest of them use other agencies. I was amazed that their agencies didn't participate or even talk on this level.

> The law firms that didn't have to pay attention to any of this before have to pay attention to it now because of the competition, so they're running scared and it's amazing.

We talked for an hour or so in a roundtable just on intake. One of my clients, who has incredibly successful, excellent lawyers, probably has the best intake procedures and accountability than almost any one of my clients. I went to Ed and I challenged him and said, "What is your abandoned call rate?" There was silence. Now, here's a group that has tracked everything and he says, "What is an abandoned call?"

Mullins: Oh, geez.

Schillinger: "What should the rate be?" The point being is that you can have the greatest systems and you can really be focused. There isn't a law firm — and I will stand my reputation on this, in fact, I'll challenge it for the fact that if I'm wrong, I'll pay for anybody's head budget for the entire year — that you can't walk in and take a good hard look at what they're doing and find an absolutely obvious way to improve it. You talked about systems and what can be done. Recently we had a meeting of our clients and I did not choose to bring in a vendor or a problem-solver in intakes. I was given three hours and I spent three hours getting my clients to recognize that they have to recognize the problem before they can go ahead and solve it.

And that is my passion. I don't have to solve the problem. I bring it to you and you solve it. I have to get my clients to recognize that they have to bring the Intake Academy into the office and recognize that they have to give their clients the tools that you are equipped to give them to solve the problem. Solving the problem is only half the equation, recognizing it is the second half. So, to come back to saying "I need you more than you need me" is when you do both. You get somebody to recognize it and you understand how to fix it.

Mullins: Right. What about the smaller firms, the smaller guys? Like the ones who might be saying, "Wow, we don't spend that kind of money but we still have the same problems." What about them?

Schillinger: Well, if I was a businessman or a lawyer and I didn't have any advertising budget or whatever, I think it still applies, because if I only got one phone call, I want to know how I handled it. Actually it applies more to people who have less money to spend because they have to spend it more wisely. The law firms that are spending millions of dollars — and I have a number of firms, at least a half-dozen firms that spend in excess of a million a year just on television — I think that this applies more to the smaller guys than the bigger guys because they have to make much more with less.

Mullins: You do support that this is for all firms? It's not just for the big guys and it's not just personal injury really, there are all types...

Schillinger: Well, I support it for any business or whatever. I just spent, literally, I think I clocked it at five hours and 47 minutes strictly on trying to get my Internet going with Comcast and I literally spoke to five people who transferred me to five different departments in three different countries and each time that I got transferred they said, "This call will be recorded for quality control." I yelled back, "What quality control? I'm not talking to anybody! Nobody is listening to me." Finally, I insisted on talking to one person in America who is a senior supervisor, and in five minutes, my problem was solved. It was a pretty big waste of my time. And, most importantly, I'm sitting here repeating how bad the situation was and I'll tell it to 20 or 30 other people.

Mullins: My last question is, seriously, what do we do about it? What can we do about it? How can we — Network Affiliates, the Intake Academy — what do we do to help?

Schillinger: Well, what I'm doing about it is I'm getting my clients to recognize the problem. And one of the best ways that I found to get them to recognize it is to give them a taste of their own medicine. I record their telephone calls and play them back because in listening to them, I'm familiar with what's going on. They truly are disconnected.

The way to connect them is to shock them and show them exactly why. It's kind of like going to the doctor and getting a tremendously bad diagnosis. You went for your annual physical and you're in shock and you say, "Well, I didn't realize I have cancer," or "I didn't realize this is such a problem. My blood pressure is so high." Getting them to recognize it is my biggest objective right now. I think that's what we all have to begin with because once they recognize it, they ask for the solution. I love bringing you in because you solve the problem — you know your business so well.

Mullins: What do you say to the law firms that are doing so well financially and they're like, "Wait, we're converting 90% of our cases." What do you say to them?

Schillinger: I say, "God bless you. I would like to cut a deal with you and just take what you're not getting and split it with you." Then they immediately say, "Well, you can't have half. You have to start to negotiate." But what do we is negotiate with regards to anything that you throw away. Now I'm picking up out of the garbage pail what you threw away, and I get their attention actually. You know, it's very difficult to tell somebody who's that financially successful that they could do so much more. But when my clients, who are doing phenomenally well, come to me and say, "I want more calls," what I do say is, "What, so you can throw out the ones I'm giving you?" You know, Chris, you wanted the unvarnished Harlan.

Mullins: Well, we certainly appreciate it. I don't have any more questions for today. Do you have anything else that you wanted to say, Harlan?

Schillinger: I think we've covered a great deal. The bottom line is that there isn't a law firm in the country that can't improve. But I do want to go back to the 94% ratio because I had a client where we converted 94% of everybody that we wanted.

Mullins: Okay.

Schillinger: There are a couple of things that you can ask the client. Number one, when they say 94% of people who they want, these are people who they spend a ton of money on to call and have determined that they want their case. They have determined that they're going to bring them into their office. When a lawyer says to you, "I convert 94% of everybody I want," that means that person is sitting across the desk from them with a fee agreement, but that's not what we're talking about today. We're talking about what they had no clue they were missing.

Mullins: Right.

Schillinger: We're talking about what they don't know. I would make a fortune by just taking the scrap that people toss away without even knowing they're tossing it away and trying to convert them. I will cut that deal with any lawyer, anywhere, any day, and please publish that.

Mullins: Oh, I'm going to. I'll share something quick. This is the way people think, or at least in my opinion. It's called the shiny object syndrome. However many years ago it was that law firms finally got it, that they actually needed to understand marketing and then not just understand it but actually do the marketing and spend money on it.

It's easy for them to just do it, to make decisions to do it, to keep going forward and they just don't look at the other pieces, like what happens when those calls come in. What are you going to do, have an insurance policy against your marketing dollars?

One day, my assistant got a phone call from a law firm. The lawyer wanted to meet with us to help him put together a script for women to read at truck stops to get the truckers to do business with them.

It's not something that we were going to do, but my point is the focus and energy, time and dollars are all spent on what's the next greatest thing. What can I do to get that phone to ring? But nobody is spending any time looking out for what happens when the phone does ring.

Schillinger: It's kind of like being single at a very young age. How many notches can I get on my bedpost as opposed to quality over quantity. And you're absolutely correct. It blows my mind when you ask how much money they spent, but most importantly, how much money has drifted away. It's amazing. Let me run something thing by you.

Mullins: Okay.

Schillinger: A lawyer gets an average of 400 calls in a month and he converts 20% of that business into cases. With an average case value of $7,500, he's going to do very well. If he increased that 20% to 22%, given the specific number that I just gave you, he will put in his pocket after advertising expenses between $350,000 to $600,000 in fees. So wouldn't it makes sense to spend the exact same amount of money on advertising and get 22% back instead of 20% back?

Mullins: Yes.

Schillinger: And the way to do that is with better conversion. Those are high dollars and if somebody doesn't quite understand that, then they're just simply making too much money.

Mullins: Absolutely.

Schillinger: I'll send you that analogy. It fits on that formula and it's beautiful because it's a fact. For every 2% that somebody spends based on that criteria, those are the percentages of return on a $7,500 case. Now, I have clients whose average case is $7,500 but I also have a client who has 3,000 cases. His average fee is $50,000 and I'm very proud to be working with that firm. It's all in the way people look at it. What I'm saying is it's all relative to what a lot of money is to somebody. I'm saying this whole conversation is based on the exact same amount of money you're spending and a much better return on your investment. That's really the bottom line.

Mullins: Right now, I can tell you from experience of listening to thousands of phone calls and looking at hundreds and hundreds of different summary call reports, anywhere between — and this is a staggering number — I would say 10 to 15% of call volume at a law firm are stranded calls. These are legitimate inbound calls, live people, not like robot spam calls, but live callers who are who are calling for help, who never make it, never talk to a live person or they get put on hold and they hang up. They never talk to a qualified person who can help them so they just go away.

Schillinger: I think the two most significant parts of abandonment... I just did an analysis on a firm and this will blow your mind. These are actual figures. I have a firm last year that had 11,500 abandoned calls. They take 10,000 calls a month, by the way, and had 11,500 abandoned calls. I look at an abandoned call as somebody who called, got put on hold for too long or got transferred too many times. So they hung up. And my question is where did they go?

Mullins: Right.

Schillinger: They went to your competitor. One of the best questions you can ask a lawyer, and I love this question, is, "Have you ever taken a call from another lawyer who turned a case down and you took it?"

Mullins: Beautiful.

Schillinger: Or his office took it. And he'll say, "Oh, absolutely, all the time." What that specifically means is that an intake specialist determined that we don't want the case or the lawyer didn't look deep enough into whether it's a good case. Now let's tighten the question up. You go ahead and ask a client, "Have you ever taken a case that another lawyer rejected and you made a six-figure fee on it?" They will say, "Oh, yes, I have." "Well, how did you get that case?" "I talked to the client and I saw something that the other lawyer didn't see or they didn't like his personality, etc." There are lots of other excuses. The fact of the matter is, it's happening to you, mister lawyer, that's happening to you every day.

Mullins: Exactly.

Schillinger: I want to get back before we close this interview as to why we feel that the unsung hero is the intake person. Firms have to recognize that person and reward that person. They have to respect that person. That person is on the firing line listening to all the problems that people have, sorting them out and bringing people in. I tell the lawyers, recognize the people who work for you. Recognize their goodwill. When an intake person goes home at night and they feel they did a good job because they took somebody's problem and gave them hope, that person drives home with a smile on their face. When that person sits down at the dining room table and says, "I helped a person get through a tough time in their life. They didn't know where to turn and I was the person that put them in the hands of a lawyer who's going to help them navigate through this big problem that they have."

We've got to recognize these people and have pride in what they do. We need to embrace them. We need to hug them and thank them and pay them. And most of all, tell them how much we appreciate them because we do underestimate them. Ask the lawyer how much you appreciate them. The lawyer thinks that because he spent the money advertising, he gets the case. But the bottom line is, they answer the phone. They connect it. They are the matchmaker and without the matchmaker, you can spend all the money in your budget. If you don't have the right person and appreciate that person answering that telephone call, you are screwed.

Mullins: Very well put. Thank you, Harlan.

Attorneys Only
Get Your FREE Mystery Call and Conversion Debrief

Go to **www.IntakeAcademy.com** and on the first page just click on *Sign Up for Free Mystery Call*. As you go through the sign-up, don't forget to schedule your **Attorney-Only** and **Chris Mullins Mystery Call Conversion Debrief**.

Never Send a Prospect to a Lawyer

When you want to return a product, do you want to talk to the marketing department or customer service? You want a direct line to the person most trained to answer your exact questions; the person who will listen and even commiserate with your frustrations about the product; the person who can facilitate returning your misfit item and reimbursing your money in the most efficient way possible.

Well, the same principle applies to taking in new cases at a law firm. Prospective clients don't want to talk to a busy, preoccupied lawyer who's deep in the research required to prepare a case. People with problems that feel very real to them — whether the predicaments turn into viable cases or not — want to talk to a qualified legal intake specialist who knows how to empathize. They want a lifeline — a person who quickly acknowledges stress and identifies with overwhelming emotions.

Often attorneys believe that they can handle it all — from intake to marketing to lawyering. But like any other business, in order to effectively service clients and build a successful organization, the experts in each line of work must handle these specialized functions. That means lawyers interpret the law. Intake specialists negotiate the calls. Marketing firms create brand strategy.

Your firm will find the quickest path to success if leadership delegates functions to the right people. Your brand counts on it. If you market your law practice as a dedicated advocate for accident victims, for example, your attorneys better be spending a large majority of their time preparing cases, negotiating settlements and trying cases in court. Not answering the phones. Not trying to qualify a case. Not designing the website. Not writing marketing copy.

After more than three decades of providing marketing and advertising expertise to firms across the country, we know that lawyers who try to do it all or micro-manage other executive functions ultimately fail. Heed our advice. Use it as a catalyst to get the right people in place before it's too late. Need help organizing your firm's functions and marketing strategies? Give Network Affiliates a call today for a complimentary evaluation at (877) 462-5184.

published 2/17/2014, Network Affiliates Blog

Arming Your Ambassador of First Impressions

Remember the last time you called customer service? Then got sent to someone overseas? That was irritating. Well, the same applies to the intake administrator for your law firm. Whether you have a large operation or one person sitting at a desk, how you take you call-in leads — and turn them into profit — matters.

If you don't have a strategy for how you handle random and strategic leads that come by phone, now is a great time to design a plan. For it's often he or she who answers the questions best who gets the case.

First, consider whether or not your intake ambassador needs a script. For firms that have the luxury of employing someone who knows the business intimately and can conversationally qualify a client, this might not be necessary. For other practices, you might have found a warm and approachable intake expert that's not quite up to speed on kinds of clients that would make a great fit.

Both scenarios require some oversight. A script or questionnaire can be a helpful aid for a person with the voice but not the knowledge. In this case, sit down to draft a conversational script that will carefully and quickly explain your firm while qualifying the caller — without closing the door too quickly. Sometimes that extra question or two can turn a borderline case into a real client.

Even if your intake person is well versed in how to answer a variety of questions from callers, it can't hurt to review this process. You never know if you could be getting more business. Consider taping intake conversations or even physically listening in on a regular basis to make sure your ambassador is asking all the questions you would were you taking to a potential client.

Remember, you spend a lot of money pleading with people to call you. Don't you think they deserve to have their expectations met when they finally do communicate with your firm? It's your responsibility to connect the dots. After all, the person who makes your firm's first impression can influence the decisions your clients make. Better hope they're good ones.

published 12/18/2013, Network Affiliates Blog

Answering the Call!

What do you spend on advertising versus answering the phone at your law office? Step back for a moment and think about how much time and money you invest in making the most effective TV advertising commercial. The point is to drive traffic and make the phone ring, right?

But what happens when the phone does ring — and all your advertising efforts start to pay off. Do you have the right people in place to make sure that those phone calls convert to cases? There are so many nuances to answering the call, from your intake professionals' tone of voice to the speed in which your office addresses inquires.

If you're wondering why your advertising is making the phone ring but cases are not growing at the rate you projected, the missing link might be a greater investment in the speed, accuracy and creativity of your call center. Here are a few questions any firm should consider when making a strategic plan for over-the-phone intake:

How knowledgeable are your call receptionists or call-center specialists about your law firm and its services?

Do they need to read from a script or can they answer on the fly a variety of questions about your legal services?

How fast do your intake professionals return a call? What happens after they've left one message for a caller?

Are you accidently turning away cases because you're not probing further into a caller's questions?

How do you handle after-hours calls?

Often the firm that's the quickest to return a call wins the case. Other cases are won by the intake representatives who are the most creative when examining a caller's legal needs — ones that might not initially fit into a firm's "box" of services. Sometimes it's the offices that have a strict policy about multiple follow-up calls that ultimately win the business. Remember, intake is not about you. It's about the caller — a busy person who has a life. And work. And kids. And can't always carve out the time to return your call within 24 hours. That doesn't mean your firm should give up trying.

If you want to increase your case load and ensure your advertising efforts have legs, start thinking more strategically about answering the call. You might find that a little fine-tuning can go a long way.

published 10/6/2013, Network Affiliates Blog

Four Tracking Tactics You Must Do

Do you monitor your 401K? How about your checkbook? Of course you track money that goes in and out of your life. Then why wouldn't you track advertising spend — one of your law firm's most significant investments?

As an ad agency, we are only as effective as our advertising campaigns. And if you don't have mechanisms in place to track who calls your firm and from where — and whether they become a client or remain a lead — you'll never know whether what you're spending is really worth it.

If you don't know what ad tactics are moving the needle, you'll never be able to make a truly informed decision about how to adjust your media mix, when to try something new or whether to ditch an unproductive effort all together.

Here are some simple examples of how we encourage our clients to track leads:

Call tracking: This can be as manual as instituting a policy to document every call that comes into your office, or as automated as installing software to record the source of each call and measure the revenue generated from each lead.

Unique tracking number: Keep track of which calls are coming from what yellow page ads by placing a unique reference number next to each ad.

Traffic analytics: Install Google Analytics or another digital tracking program to monitor how visitors found your website — organic search, online referral source, PPC ad — as well as what keyword they used to search for you, how long they stayed and what pages they hit.

Microsite or PPC campaign: Generate stronger Web leads by building an exclusive landing page or mini website for a specific mass tort, for example, or other area of your practice you want to grow. Online campaigns are highly trackable often yield near-instant ROI.

Ultimately, advertising translates to paid leads. To see what you're really spending per lead, simply divide your advertising budget by the number of leads you've tracked — in a week, month or year. Compare your expenditures on advertising campaigns and you'll quickly see what's working and what needs tweaking.

published 3/14/2013, Network Affiliates Blog

Testimonials

Harlan Schillinger has taken the marketing activities and results for dozens of litigation law firms in America to a higher and vastly superior plateau. His remarkable insight makes him the best, but his extraordinary vision makes it work for his clients. Harlan has such a warm and personal hands-on approach, yet is full of energy and enthusiasm at every stage of helping others to realize dreams and goals. He so totally recognizes that boosting you and your firm helps your clients, your staff, your family and our system of justice. Harlan took our firm to marketing levels we through were unreachable!

John F. Romano, West Palm Beach, FL

Harlan has been in the forefront of legal advertising for 30 years and I've worked with him since 1994. He was instrumental in helping us develop new market strategies during the years when competition among lawyers became fierce and new avenues for reaching out to our client base began to arise. He was always a step ahead, and always fun to work with.

Len Jacoby, Jacoby and Meyers

I have known Harlan for over thirty years; Harlan knows how to turn a prospect into a client cost effectively.

Jim Sokolove, Sokolove Law, Boston, MA

I have had the privilege to work with Harlan Schillinger and his team at Network Affiliates on numerous legal marketing projects over the past 12 years. Harlan's knowledge of legal marketing and advertising continued to be ahead of the industry, and his insight for creative work always resulted in new opportunities. Thank you, Harlan, for always pushing me to see new perspectives.

Keith Givens, Cochran Firm, Dothan, AL

I have known and worked with Harlan for more than twenty years. He is a great friend and adviser who brings integrity and passion to everything he does. His depth of knowledge about marketing and advertising for attorneys is beyond compare and, most importantly, Harlan gets outstanding results for his clients.

Dan Goldstein, Page 1 Solutions

Harlan Schillinger is a visionary in the world of legal advertising. His keen insight based on years of experience provides his clients with the ability to achieve a successful advertising campaign in the competitive world of lawyer advertising. His integrity and willingness to share ideas makes Harlan a rare colleague and advisor when it is important to make strategic advertising decisions. I value Harlan's friendship and bounce ideas off of him on a regular basis with the utmost confidence in his marketing experience and expertise.

Arthur Elk

As one of the largest legal advertisers in America, and having done this for over 30 years, I have seen my share of so called "experts" come and go. Harlan is one of the few consultants that actually gets it! His ideas are solid, and he understands the strategies of successful advertising which he has proven time and time again over the years.

Morris Bart, Morris Bart, LLC, First Bank & Trust Tower

Harlan is a genius when it comes to marketing law firms. He has always shared freely with me his ideas and strategies on effective and innovative ways to general new leads. Thanks for sharing your vast wealth of knowledge.

Attorney Ken Hardison, www.Pilmma.org

Harlan knows legal advertising, he knows the players and more importantly he knows how to play the game. We have been very pleased with the service and creative products we have received from his company and I would not hesitate to recommend him and Network to my friends. I appreciate the knowledge and experience they bring to the table.

Michael DeMayo, Managing Principal and President of DeMayo Law

Harlan possesses understanding of legal advertising that is unparalleled. He has developed relationships throughout the country, and his broad knowledge base and national scope of his contacts allow him to offer "value added" legal advertising support to his clients. Harlan is part of a superb team of advertising professionals at Network Affiliates, and we are proud to be associated with them.

John Sakson, Co-Managing Partner at Stark & Stark

AHA Notes:

Resource: To get more information on International Intake Specialist Week™, the Legal Intake Specialist Association™ (LISA) Boot Camp and Legal Intake Specialist 911™, call (603) 924-1640 or email beth@intakeacademy.com. Refer to page 176 in this book.

About Chris Mullins

Chris Mullins, an entrepreneur and business owner for more than 25 years, is the Phone Sales Doctor™ and CEO of the Intake Academy™ LLC, a division of Mullins Media Group™ LLC, and has helped hundreds of companies improve their use of the telephone through mystery call shopping with a special focus on the architecture of the script, script review, sales and staff coaching. Chris is an expert at dramatically increasing appointments (sales) from your existing incoming calls. She is legendary for coaching law firms, intake specialists, attorneys, case managers and all types of business owners and sales professionals to "No Excuses" peak productivity. Chris Mullins and the team of in-house certified coaches, with the clients' permission, listen to your phone calls to design an incoming and outbound sales call script for you that is easy to implement and instantly makes you more money.

The Intake Academy offers strategies and training for intake specialists, lawyers, paralegals, call center agents, receptionists and business owners to grow their firm by converting more callers to qualified cases, rapidly qualifying good cases and transforming unqualified prospects to advocates for your firm — whether you're able to handle their case or not. You'll discover how to cement relationships with more of your ideal clients, get them to commit to you and send you more referrals than you every thought possible. We focus on five areas:

1) Relationships first, business second

2) Consistent, integrity-based sales process

3) Empowering and enabling staff with right skills

4) Ongoing coaching and reinforcement to ensure intake quality

5) Intake specialist hiring, screening and selection

Take the Intake Academy First Impressions Directors' Oath

I, Chris Mullins, the first impressions director (first responder), receptionist, front desk team member will go to any length to absolutely make sure all client and prospective client phone calls are taken care of correctly. I understand that the real purpose of my job is to be the advocate for every single phone call and to protect each call. I have been empowered to do whatever is necessary to guarantee that each call safely arrives in the hands of the next team member. I will uphold this oath to whatever length is necessary.

To learn more, call (603) 924-1640 *or visit* www.IntakeAcademy.com.

Chapter One

*Interviews With Our
Five Intake Super Heroes*

Five Intake Specialist Super Heroes
Real Lives, Real Stories of the Unsung Heroes of Law Firms Worldwide

To protect the privacy of our intake specialist heroes, we have not published their real names or firm names. The stories you're about to read are very real and I personally found it to be emotionally challenging to remain composed during each interview. I am very proud of each hero who was interviewed. You are very brave, strong and incredibly gifted individuals. Thank you for this opportunity to step into each of your lives. *– Chris Mullins*

Chris Mullins Interviews Hero #1

Mullins: So, are you nervous?

Hero #1: A little bit.

Mullins: You'll be fine. It's just you and me. How long have you been working there now? I think you said two or three years?

Hero #1: Yes, two-and-a-half, almost three.

Mullins: Again, we won't publish your name or the name of the firm. Do you remember why you took the job?

Hero #1: Yes, I do. I was actually very excited to come over here to work with people who need help, need our assistance moving forward. I personally like talking to people and trying to help people. Why I really decided to move over... at my last job I was there for five years and I did enjoy it, but I just wasn't as engaged with clients as I have the opportunity to be here.

Mullins: But prior to that, you were at another business?

Hero #1: Yes.

Mullins: Okay, because you said you moved over. I thought maybe you were in another department or something.

Hero #1: Oh, no. I've always been within this department. My roles have changed a little bit throughout the years. But I've always been within the same area of the firm since I've started.

Mullins: What kind of job did you have before you came to the firm?

Hero #1: I was in insurance sales.

Mullins: Oh, boy.

Hero #1: It's very stressful.

Mullins: Was it all on the phone or did you have to go out on the road?

Hero #1: Not on the road but we did marketing within the city. No out of town travel, but within the city and face-to-face. We do have clients that come in. We had an office. So we had clients that came in and it wasn't over the phone mainly. Our main point of contact was in person.

Mullins: Right. But five years? That's a long time.

Hero #1: Yes. It is a long time.

Mullins: Sales is tough — it's just tough. I think it's tough depending on the business that you work in. Do you know what I mean?

Hero #1: Yes.

Mullins: I know why you took the job. How do you feel two-and-a-half years later about what you're doing now?

Hero #1: I still love being here, being able to help people, talk to people, speak with people. We are making a difference in their lives. Yes, at times it is very stressful as call volume increases, but overall, I do enjoy coming to work. I look forward to being here, being on the phone waiting for the next call, making sure that we're doing everything that we can to help them in the long run. I still enjoy it even though it has been a couple of years. It's never to the point where I dread coming in, although there are some days that are a little more stressful than others. But at the end of the day, I still enjoy working here. And I try to convey that when I work.

Mullins: Okay.

Hero #1: I do like what I do and I think we have a good company that really does care generally about the people we are working for.

Mullins: Let's talk about the difficult stuff. In other words, even for me, I've been doing what I'm doing for 25 years now and I still have days when there's a meltdown.

Hero #1: Sure.

Chapter 1: *Interviews With Our Five Intake Super Heroes*

Mullins: It happens to all of us. So what's it like for you? As a reminder for you, the purpose for me talking to you right now is I want intake specialists, front desk receptionists in law firms, worldwide, to read what it's like. The good and the bad for their colleagues and all these other firms to help them feel better about what they do and to remind themselves that they are heroes, that what they do is so important and it shouldn't be taken lightly.

But also I'm doing this book because I want business owners, partners, the principles of the firm to have another opportunity to remind themselves of how critically important the intake specialists are to the practice.

So, what about those days when your worst phone call happens? What's the worst phone call that you've ever had that you can remember? What's that person saying to you?

Hero #1: Well, yesterday was particularly bad and I haven't had one in those in a while. It wasn't me who was speaking with the client, but they were irate. Unfortunately, we were not able to help that particular individual. We are applying for benefits to the Social Security System and they have set specifications on who qualifies and who doesn't. There's no way around that. If they exceed a particular resource for a particular program, there is nothing else that we can do. We're filing it through the federal system.

So unfortunately, for this client, at first when we extended a welcome representation, "Yes, we can help you," we then come to find out we couldn't help him after some other information was disclosed later on down the road. He was very upset wondering why this wasn't brought up to begin with and was cussing on the line.

Mullins: Really?

Hero #1: He wanted to fire us. This just happened yesterday. We had already made up the paperwork so that we could become his representatives. We received it but we were not able to process and actually get that submitted to the Social Security Administration. He just wanted closure at that point because now we're gathering more information. We're getting all of these components in and now we're realizing, "You know what? I'm sorry. We're not going to be able help you after all. We were not aware of XYZ in the beginning. Now that we are, there's nothing else that we can do about it." So, he was very upset.

That was, you know, particularly stressful and, of course, on our end we don't want that to happen. We always want to make them understand that we are trying to help them. There are just some points where we cannot override what the requirements are or what the limitations are on those types of applications.

At the end of the day we were able to get him to calm down a little bit and explain it to him. He did have a good understanding as to why we were not able to move forward for his particular case and help them, so it was ultimately resolved but during that phone call it was very stressful. If I wasn't here, I wouldn't understand either. "You said you can help me. Now three weeks down the road, you're saying you can't. What happened? What changed?" We have to explain that to him and ultimately we did. It was just that the process was a little tedious.

Mullins: It sounds like the phone call took a long time. How were you able to calm this person down?

Hero #1: It did take a long time. What we did was the first individual who spoke with him, the person who got the call, had actually talked to him previously. She had talked to him the day before and she let him know, "We're going to wait for a little bit more information where we just want to be sure that we're not giving you any type of wrong information. Once we get a particular letter, we're going to follow up with you and make sure that we understand the information that you're telling us is exactly what the Social Security Administration has seen."

We want to confirm with the notice that they're going to issue. That was the first day of the call when we were brought the other information. The next day, he called again and the same individual took the call still trying to work it out for him. When she could no longer just speak with the client or relay that information to him, we did have to have a manager step in and help with that call.

Mullins: Okay. For yourself, have you ever had to ask anybody if they've tried to commit suicide?

Hero #1: Yes, I have.

Mullins: We listen to so many phone calls at the Intake Academy. We've heard terrible things with all different clients, not necessarily your firm in particular, but all clients. What's that like when you have to ask that question? How is that for you?

Hero #1: It's very personal. You want to try to make them as comfortable as you can because, for example, I'm a very private person. I would not want to disclose that. I wouldn't want to tell somebody else any type of information I've got on myself. We just want to make them feel with the information they're giving that we are handling this and we are ultimately asking these types of questions to help them. We want to be sure that the applications we are doing for them, this may help quicken the process of an ultimate decision.

Yes, it is personal and we try to empathize with them and make sure that they know we do care for them as a person and that we do appreciate them speaking with us about sensitive topics. In the long run, this is going to be something that is going to help them.

Mullins: So, when you get ready to ask that to somebody that question, it's never easy, right?

Hero #1: No.

Mullins: I'm sure you've had people say, "Yes, I've tried." What about people who say that and they start to tell you their whole story? What's that like?

Hero #1: At times we do get emotional with clients. We want to, of course, be professional, but it does take a toll when these clients are trusting you with their private life, with their personal information. So we try to remain calm, be very sympathetic, empathetic, sincere and, of course, gather the information we need. We don't want to brush them off or rush on to the next subject or next question. You know, take a moment to let them explain.

And there are times where they let you know, "I can't go any further." And that's okay. We're like, "Thank you. You're doing great. I appreciate what you have told me thus far." I'll try moving along to a different subject and then maybe we can come back and feel a little better. I try to make sure that their needs are taking care of.

Mullins: I'm sure that you've had times when people have maybe asked you or looked at you as a resource like, "What should I do? I want to kill myself." Do you ever get people who think that you are going to talk them through a problem like that?

Hero #1: At times they will mention it but, of course, we're not professionals and we do have numbers to give them, aides that can help them. If we think that they are in severe risk, then we can actually transfer them over to somebody that can help them, whether it's 911 if they've already hurt themselves or a suicide hotline. We have those numbers.

Mullins: Okay.

Hero #1: We don't need to let them know that we are not professionals in that manner but we can help them find the help that they need.

Mullins: But how do you deal with these kinds of phone calls, whether it's people talking about suicide or not? As a person, I know you're doing what you're doing because you want to help people and I understand that and I believe that. But at the end of the day, how the heck do you get through all of those calls and then get in a car and go home to your family?

Hero #1: Well, I try to the best I can... you know, take a deep breath, just relax and try not to let that affect my home life. Of course there are times you need to bend a little bit. Sometimes even just talking with a co-worker. We're all in this together.

Mullins: That's right.

Hero #1: At the end of the day or the next day, we've been trying to do huddles so that we can talk to each other and know that we have peers here that can help each other. We have a very involved management staff as well. In our department we are doing huddles because we find that they help, especially with the type of applications that are very personal. They do give a lot of private information like that and it can be very stressful when they start telling you what they've been through and then they thank you.

Mullins: It's really hard. It doesn't really matter, you know, especially the field that you're in but really, all types of law, even personal injury. The kinds of phone calls that you are taking every day all day long, it's really difficult. Do you have a family? Do you have children or are you by yourself?

Hero #1: I do have a family. I have two children and so that means I'm with them going outside to get some fresh air. Music helps also. Now that spring is here, starting in the baseball field, just to be outside, be with them and try to let some of that stress and energy out.

Mullins: When you're on your way to work, do you have a ritual or a routine or something that you do emotionally or mentally to get yourself ready to walk into the building? Or do you go and take it as it comes?

Hero #1: I just go with it. I already know on Mondays that it's usually going to be our busiest day.

Mullins: Really?

Hero #1: Usually Mondays are the toughest day in the week.

Mullins: Well, I think that you're amazing. I'm speaking to you because what you do is so important and the fact that you're part of this book to help other people who do what you do to realize, hey, this is a gift that you have that you're giving to all of these people on the phone.

You don't want to take it lightly, but you also need to take care of yourself and make sure that you do the huddle or ask for help or raise your hand or take a break, whatever you have to do. At the end of the day, my hope for you is that you really realize what a gift it is that you have and what you're doing every day on every single phone call. I'm really proud of you.

Hero #1: Oh, thank you, I appreciate it. You brought up a lot of key points in our Intake Academy training that we are taking into account, you know, the breaks, the time off, the huddles, the grouping, the script is great. These are things that are helping us grow as people, as a firm, as a department and helping us through those tough calls.

Mullins: So my last question for you is what would you say to other intake specialists, because every firm calls what you do something different. Some firms say intake specialist, some say application, some say visibility, some say front desk, reception, call center, client services. There's a different name for all kinds of firms, believe it or not. What would you say to them, the people who feel like they just can't take it anymore and what they're doing is not important?

Hero #1: I would say that is definitely not true. For every one upset client, there are probably 20 that have benefitted from your conversation with them, from you just being there to talk to them, to speak with them, to let them know that they are being cared for. That is what is going to help you in the long run. Yes, there are some days that are more stressful than others, but it's not like that every day. There are a lot more good times than bad.

Mullins: You just keep going. You just keep doing the good things you're doing and keep giving your gift to every person you speak to — even on a Monday. Don't sit back. Stand a lot taller, if you're standing tall now, stand even taller. I think that you're a true leader for your team.

Hero #1: Thank you.

Mullins: And your name will be part of the raffle for the donation. Everybody's name who gets interviewed in all these different practices will be in the raffle. Whoever's name is chosen, we're going to make a five-hundred dollar donation to their favorite charity in their name.

Hero #1: That's awesome.

Mullins: Keep up the good work.

Chris Mullins' Challenge: Hold your intake specialists accountable for taking their scheduled breaks. Set up an Intake Academy venting lounge or quiet room and make sure everyone has water and healthy snacks at their desk all day long. Have scheduled stretch sessions, even if it's a timer that goes off on the computer. For five minutes stand up and stretch, do yoga at your desk time. You can even hire (very inexpensively) an outside yoga instructor to have several scheduled basic yoga sessions throughout the day. Coach your intake team to attend the sessions — even if it's only for 10 minutes. To learn more about the Intake Academy wellness program, email beth@intakeacademy.com and put HERO WELLNESS in the subject line.

Chris Mullins Interviews Hero #2

Mullins: I wanted to interview you because not only are you amazing, but you're an intake specialist for a call center that services law firms. The purpose of the book is because I feel that you, all of you folks, that take these phone calls, whether Social Security or mass tort or personal injury, whatever the area of law it is, you're getting those calls. It's really tough not just because of the amount of calls that you get, but mostly because of the type of calls that you get.

It's hard to navigate these calls but it's also hard emotionally for you, let's say, to deal with some of the terrible things that you're hearing and then just have to move on to the next one. I want to shine a light on people like you that do this job because I think if you can share the good, the bad, the ugly — you know, your story — then it will help other intake specialists to realize, "Hey, I'm not alone. I can learn from what that person just said or what I read from them."

It puts a bigger magnifying glass on the intake specialist and makes them become much more important by giving them the spotlight. So, those are the reasons we're doing it.

Hero #2: Thank you.

Mullins: How long have you been taking inbound phone calls for law firms?

Hero #2: I've been working with the company for about eight years, specifically specializing in intakes for about five years now.

Mullins: What can you remember, off the top of your head, that's the worst experience you had with, let's say, somebody being really mean or abusive over the phone to you?

Hero #2: The situations really vary. I try not so much to focus on the bad so it's hard to give a specific idea of when something has happened. I know in our profession we take calls like that on a daily basis. Probably the worst thing that I've ever been through would be somebody who's really upset, but by trying to work with them and understanding their situation, the end result usually ends up being positive.

Mullins: Say you're in the middle of someone yelling at you or swearing at you and calling you names. Does that ever happen?

Hero #2: I've had situations like that but I've usually been able to work through them and end up getting a good result with the situation and so forth.

Mullins: How do you work through them if that happens?

Hero #2: Usually, that's the one thing that people are the most upset about — somebody not listening to them. They have been trying to get this assistance, they've been trying to get help and nobody is responding. No one is contacting them. No one is just listening to them.

I find that by sitting there and listening to somebody and confirming their situation and understanding where it is that they're coming from and why they're frustrated usually ends up with a good result by sitting there and saying, "You know, I understand where you're coming from and I'm really sorry that this has happened and that you haven't heard back from anybody. I'm going to do my best."

I'll generally give them my name and my word that I'm going to do everything I can to try to get them the help that they need right now. Usually when that happens, most people end up being more responsive and it ends in a good result with them saying, "You know, thank you for your help," towards the end of the call when it may not have started out so well.

Mullins: What about you as a person, as an individual, is it hard? Even though you're trying to diffuse the situation, and it sounds like more times than not you're probably successful, but what about you as a person separate from your career, maybe even when you first started your career. Is it hard for you to hear and be talked to that way?

Hero #2: I don't think it's ever easy for someone to be talked to that way. Maybe towards the beginning it used to really hurt. There are days, of course, when you do feel like crying. The longer you do it, though, the more you realize it's not that they're mad at you, they're mad about the situation or something that's happened to them that led up to this situation for them being so upset or so angry that's causing them to call in and be so frustrated.

Mullins: But you know what? Just to kind of interrupt you for a second. I understand all that and I know that's where you've come to. But here you are, maybe you've only been on a job for a year or two. Try to put yourself back to when you first started. Only you'll know, but when you're taking phone calls like that, everybody has good and bad days.

On the bad days, when you used to be or when you still are really emotional about it, it's really hard for you to hear somebody saying these things and then to wipe them away and say, "It's not really me." The days that you're not strong or that you used to not be strong with getting through that, what made you stay in the job?

Now, when I ask that question to people like you, some will say, "To be honest, Chris, I had to keep food in the table." Some will say something totally different. But what keeps you in that kind of job, in that kind of environment?

Hero #2: I really care. I don't know, but I genuinely care about everyone. In this position, there's only so much that you can do to help people, but sometimes just being there in that moment and taking the abuse or sitting there and listening to somebody, you end up helping them. Even if it's over the phone and just hearing that somebody cares. I want people to know that someone does care about them and that they're not alone.

Mullins: Okay. Do you take Social Security calls?

Hero #2: We do take Social Security.

Mullins: Do you personally take them?

Hero #2: Yes. I personally take Social Security Disability intake calls.

Mullins: Okay. So… if I have to ask you to repeat something it's just because you're on a conference call and sometimes it's hard to hear but you're doing a great job. Have you ever had phone calls where somebody would be like, "I'm going to kill myself, or I've tried to kill myself," or anything like that?

Hero #2: I did one time. It wasn't necessarily for the Social Security Disability. But it was in a different type of account. When that happens I just try to stay on the phone with them and I try to get them the help that they need. It ended up getting them to a counselor but that was very scary. It was very emotional to sit there and be scared that someone was going to hurt themselves while you're on the phone with them.

Mullins: What were they saying?

Hero #2: They were stating that they had a gun and that they wanted to shoot themselves. They were saying that, "You know, this is the end. I can't do this anymore." I remember sitting there and in my head thinking nothing is ever so bad that you can't want to do it anymore. You have to stay strong and you have to want to be here. And maybe those things shouldn't have been said but I did tell them, "You know, you need to stay strong. You need to stick with it. Nothing can be so bad that you want to take your life away because then it can't get better. Things always have a way of getting better."

Mullins: The other day I was listening to some real phone calls from some of our clients and the very first thing this woman said when she called this law firm was, "My sister is dying of cancer any day now. I need to get some help." That was the very first thing that she said. Have you gotten calls like that? Maybe not cancer, maybe something else like, "My child was just hit by a car," things like that.

Hero #2: There's one call that will always stay with me but still even the fact that it's done, I do wonder how she's doing. There was a lady who called in on a personal injury law firm. She had a child and her child had passed. It was a very unfortunate situation. Her child was in his teens. She said there was this hole. There were no signs blocking off the property and he ended up going into the hole and the rope broke and he died.

The police department made out like it was his fault that he shouldn't have been there. She was just getting the whole run-around and the whole time this poor lady is like, "I'm just trying to get help." Supposedly that area was considered to be off limits but the signs were missing and nothing had been posted up.

> Chris, my advice to law firms would be just to take a moment and call back clients to let them know that you're still looking into it, that you're still researching, that you're still looking at it and that you care about them versus never calling them back.

Mullins: When you took that phone call and she told you that story, what was that like?

Hero #2: I ended up getting off the phone with her, I did have to take a moment because I'm a mother and just the thought of something like that happening, I had to take a moment. I had to go back and take a couple of moments to recuperate. I was crying even while I was on the phone with her, I did have tears running down my face.

Mullins: Of course.

Hero #2: For that type of situation though, sometimes you have to take a moment to turn off, regroup your thoughts and then be ready for the next new situation that's coming your way.

Mullins: I get it and I hear you. But how the heck do you do it? Especially if you're in an environment where you get a lot of calls and they're coming at you one after another? How do you keep going? What happens when you get in the car and you go home at night? As you're driving home, are you thinking about everything or did you immediately shut it off? How does it affect you with your family?

Hero #2: Honestly, you have to shut it off. You can't take it with you because if you take it with you, it would just be too much. I honestly just take one call at a time. Every situation has its own demand and if I were to take everything home… I would probably say my stress level has definitely been high since I started here eight years ago. I definitely have a lot more stress, but I just try to take my time to breathe, to refresh and then when I'm home, I'm home. When I'm at work, it's work.

> Chris, so many firms put so much time and effort into getting those potential clients. But what about keeping their existing clients?

Mullins: When you drive in to work for the start of your day, like when you get out of bed in the morning, do you start thinking about work or do you not think about it until you're in the car or do you not think about it until you get in the building?

Hero #2: I probably say I think about work 24 hours. I don't always talk about it. And I have dreams about work.

Mullins: What kinds of dreams?

Hero #2: Just various different situations, getting that call where you just can't help or can't fix something. Feeling bad about those people who you repeatedly speak with and they're constantly telling you, "Nobody is helping me. No one is giving me a call back." Call center-wise I'd have to say that's probably the hardest thing to deal with because there's only so much that you can do to help them.

Mullins: Right.

Hero #2: And when you speak with them time and time again and you hear nobody is helping them, that's probably the hardest thing that I personally have to deal with on a daily basis. If I could give any advice to a law firm, it'd be just to take a moment and call back clients to let them know that you're still looking into it, that you're still researching, that you're still looking at it and that you care about them versus never calling them back or telling them anything.

Mullins: So, your advice for law firms is to make sure that they have people in place, to just keep calling and communicating even if you can't give the news that someone wants to hear.

Hero #2: Just to communicate, that's all people want. They want to know what's happening. Even if they're an existing client, I know so many firms put so much time and effort into getting those potential clients. But what about keeping their existing clients? Those existing clients are just as important, and not following up or even taking a moment to say, "Hey, I just wanted to check in to let you know I'm still looking into it. But I promise that I'll contact you as soon as I know."

Mullins: Right. Let me ask you this. And don't forget, today – I don't know if you know this or not, but today at 3:00 EST — I think that's probably 12:00 for you guys — is the staff question and answer phone call with me. I don't know if you know that or not.

Hero #2: No, I didn't know.

Mullins: I'll give you the conference line and see if it's okay for you to attend. But it's the staff only question and answer phone call with Chris Mullins. It's for all of our law firms. It's just for staff, the receptionist, the intake specialist — people like you that are handling the calls.

It's only for an hour but they jump on and you don't have to say who you are if you don't want to. It's very informal and you can jump on and ask me a question. You can listen to everybody else. You can help somebody, that sort of thing.

If you had the power to help intake specialists at law firms or call centers... If you were the CEO, the one that could make the decision, what do you think intake specialists need? What service or resource or support or coaching — what kind of help do you think would be great for the intake specialist — what do you think they need to help themselves get through their job? What do you think would be a great idea? Have you ever thought of it?

Hero #2: I think having a general knowledge of the types of people who are contacting you, that's the number one most important thing because you need to be prepared to answer those difficult questions, not necessarily legal questions, but those difficult questions that people are calling in to seek advice. They need that reassurance. They need to know that you are going to help them and that they did the right thing in contacting you.

I personally think from hearing other calls and from seeing and hearing things from other people is empathy. You honestly need to care about that caller. You need to go into it wholeheartedly and try to help them, not just sit there and be like, "I'm going to get the information and do what I have to do."

No, you need to really sit there and listen to them and tell them that you understand and that you do care about why they're calling and not just get the information and get them off the line.

Mullins: For example, 911 has a call center. I don't know if you ever heard me talk about or if you remember me talking about venting lounges, but they have a room that they call the quiet room. And when somebody is on a 911 call, you can imagine those calls, right? If they're on the phone and if they can't take it, if they can't handle the pressure of that call or even when they're done with the call, they can raise their hand, there's always a supervisor that can see them. They immediately go into the quiet room and somebody sits in their place. It's a way for them to get a timeout immediately. So those are things that I want you to think about. Can you do that?

Hero #2: I can.

Mullins: Well, I think you're awesome. I'm proud of you. I wish I was there right now to give you a hug. I was not having the best morning or the best week — I'm human too. My morning wasn't exactly what I had planned it to be until I talked to you.

Hero #2: Thank you, Chris. I appreciate that.

Mullins: My pleasure. Bye now.

Hero Update

Just before we went to press, we received this update from Hero #2.

Good morning Chris,
Here is my answer for the question you asked. Knowledge is power. The more you know about the subject the better you are able to under-

stand what is needed to do a good intake. I feel that providing hands-on learning/training for your team is a must in this field.

Intake specialists should have weekly meetings to discuss situations they've had and get input from their peers. I feel it's important to provide immediate feedback and to have someone there to answer questions along the way. In order to truly understand where someone is coming from, you need to teach your intake specialists to put themselves in the caller's shoes.

I would explain the importance of understanding where your caller is coming from and to imagine how you would feel if this were happening to you. I would tell them to never be quick to judge someone or a situation; you need to have all the facts before coming to a conclusion. I would provide a safe place for employees to recover from hard calls and to take a moment to clear their mind.

I feel that having these items in place for employees would help them succeed and improve the overall intake process for a firm.

Chris Mullins Interviews Hero #3

Mullins: Thank you for this interview. The purpose of the book is I want to shine a very bright light on intake specialists in law firms worldwide.

Hero #3: Right.

Mullins: One of the reasons we want to do this book is because it's just amazing what you do but I don't really feel like all intake specialists realize how wonderful they are or how important it is what they do. I don't think all of them really understand how they positively touch so many lives every single day..

I also don't feel that the lawyers, the partners, the senior level executives in the law firms understand. I want you to know that I take this interview very seriously and together we can turn intake specialists into celebrities worldwide. The people who are going to read this book are going to be intake specialists. People who have been doing the job for years, maybe some that are brand new, maybe some that aren't quite sure if they should take the job or if they should keep the job. Your interview will be helping everyone.

Hero #3: Okay.

Mullins: How long have you been an intake specialist?

Hero #3: Six years.

Mullins: In one location?

Hero #3: Yes.

Mullins: Okay. Try to remember back when you took the job, however long ago it was, what was going on in your life that made you take this job?

Hero #3: Well, I wanted to do something different, to see what other gifts that I had inside, you know, to step out of my box, because I used to be an aerobic instructor and a personal trainer. I wanted to move in another direction. So when I got hired here, it just opened up my world to... how can I say it? The world out there is such a hurting world and I said, "Man, I really love this job. I like to help people."

Mullins: Right.

Hero #3: It really gave me an understanding of how many people out there have problems and are hurting. I thought, "This is a perfect job for me." That's why I stayed this long.

Mullins: Okay. Think about... you don't have to give me specific details or names of anything or anyone, but I know because I've listened to thousands of real recorded calls every month from law firms across the country of all different sizes. I hear all the terrible stories. Think about one of the terrible experiences that you had on the phone with the prospective client. What was their story that just made you hang on for dear life so that you could help them get through it?

Hero #3: Oh, one in particular was a family member that called in. And I tell you what, when I listen to the story, my heart... I actually had to hold my tears back because I had to be strong for that person. But one in particular was when the person — she was a wife but the brother was calling — was in the building and it blew up. She was burned over 90% of her body and ended up passing away.

But the urgency to gather the information and to get an attorney to assist in this situation, that to me was the most dramatic because the woman had a 5-year-old son. And that broke my heart, you know, so that was the most dramatic.

It was a situation where there was an explosion and her whole body was burned but the thing is that when he called, he says, "You know what? Another family member was with her, and her body ended up blowing up in the air and it was just a horrible experience, you know." The other person didn't make it either but the fact that this woman had a 5-year-old son and he had to be told that his mother passed away... Now the little boy does not have his mother.

Mullins: What about when you were in the middle of listening to her brother? How did you keep it together to take care of that call?

Hero #3: Well, when I was speaking to him he was pretty shaken up. He wanted to make sure that we were able to assist with this case and I was with him all the way. I told him, "We're going to go ahead and assist you. I'm so sorry that this has happened. My heart goes out to you." I told him I would get an attorney on the phone right away as soon as we finished with the information. I told him that he's not alone and that whatever we can do to assist him with that situation, we're going to do. But I had to remain strong even when he was telling me how she was injured and the condition that she was in.

I was overcome with emotion but I could not cry on the phone even though my heart wanted to. I had to remain strong. He was reaching out to me and my hand was reaching out to him. It's almost like I was with him in the experience the whole time. That's how I felt, like I was going through everything with him. We ended up assisting him. I got an attorney to help calm him down, to make sure that we were going to go ahead and assist him. I told him I'm so glad that he called our law firm, that he made the right decision to call. I told him, "Please keep me posted on how you're doing." I always like to put that in there to make it like a relationship like, "We're here, whatever questions you have feel free to call me." And he kept in touch a little bit and then I don't know what happened after that. But I hope that everything went well.

Mullins: When you had the phone call with him, was it one phone call?

Hero #3: It was one phone call and after that he called me several times later and thanked me. And I told him to just call anytime if there's anything else that we can do. He called me about two more times and that was it. But I was telling him that he made the best decision in calling our law firm. He was pretty traumatized.

Mullins: Right.

Hero #3: Granted, he was crying but I told him that we are here for him. I made him feel that we are here for him and I meant it.

Mullins: When you were on the phone, how long of a phone conversation was it, roughly?

Hero #3: Well, in a situation like this because there are a lot of emotions involved, you don't want to rush.

Mullins: Right.

Hero #3: The conversation probably took around, let's say, 20 minutes at the most, and by the time I got an attorney to call him, you're looking at about 25 minutes. Those are delicate calls.

Mullins: Oh, sure.

Hero #3: You want to make sure that you are there with them and you're not rushing them off because the first call is the most important I believe. It's like the first impression. I wanted to make sure that we held his hand.

Mullins: Have you ever had a conversation with somebody that says, "Look, I'm going to kill myself," you know, a suicide type of thing? How the heck do you deal with it?

Hero #3: I had a call like that one time where she wanted an attorney on the phone because she was overcome with emotion. I told her, "You know, ma'am, take a good deep breath. You have to think about your family." I asked her how many children she has, and she says, "I have five." "You have to think about them. You're very important and we're glad that you called this law firm."

She felt better, but she was overcome with emotion. She was happy that she called our law firm. It was a situation we were not able to assist her in because we're personal injuries. But I referred her to where she was able to get some kind of assistance.

Mullins: Here's another question for you. When you wake up in the morning, before you get out of bed, when if at all do you start thinking about work or the types of phone calls you're going to get that day? Do you start when you wake up? Do you start when your feet touch the floor? Do you start when you're driving or do you start when you sit at your desk?

Hero #3: Actually when I start driving to work. I get prepared, go over the script. I do. I say to myself, "How can I answer this question? How can I be more effective this way?" So I start to talk to myself on the way to work. That way I'm better prepared when I'm here. Of course, I say a little prayer so I can assist whoever calls. But I feel that every call is very important. Chris, I do have your rock on my desk and I have a hand reaching out. As they reach out to me, I reach out to them. That's what I think — that they're reaching out to me. Then I'm going to go ahead and reach out to them.

> That's what I think — that they're reaching out to me. Then I'm going to go ahead and reach out to them.

Mullins: So the rock helps you to do that?

Hero #3: Yes, I have a picture in front of my desk of my rock.

Mullins: What about at night time when you're done with work, you've had a long day or a long week. That's hard enough as it is, but they're hard emotional sad kinds of stories that are true.

Hero #3: Yes.

Mullins: How do you shut it off when you go home to your family?

Hero #3: Well, when I go home, everything is in my car. I do think about all the calls that I took and especially those that are heartbreaking. I say a prayer for them. I say, "Lord, help that person, whatever they need. Just be there for them." And I say that as I go home. When I get home, my husband already has the meal and everything ready and I have the fish and the dog to take care of so they consume my time. But when I lay down, I do think about those people and that's how I actually pray for them. That brings me great peace in my heart that at least someone is praying for them. That's how I cope with it.

> But when I lay down, I do think about those people and that's how I actually pray for them. That brings me great peace in my heart that at least someone is praying for them. That's how I cope with it.

Mullins: Well, they're fortunate to have you, for sure. Let's pretend that you are the CEO of the firm. You're in charge, you're the decision maker. You can do whatever you want. If you were the person that could make changes and decisions at your firm to help the intake specialists, to give them more support whether it'd be coaching or venting or breaks... I'll give you quick example. The people at 911, they take calls all day long.

Hero #3: Yes.

Mullins: Emergency calls, like they don't know what kind of call they're going to get either. They work in a call center just like you do. In the 911 environment, if an agent takes a call and they're having a hard time with a call, when that call is done, they can raise their hand and there are supervisors all over constantly. As soon as someone sees their hand raised, they have a room, a private lounge room that's called the quiet room. They get to go in there by themselves and be alone and somebody else sits in their chair to take the calls.

So if you were the person that can make the decision to support or help or guide even more the people who take these calls, what would you do? What ideas do you have? Does anything ever come to mind?

What do you think would be great for a law firm, what service could a law firm provide to actual people like you, an intake specialist, that's on the phone all day long taking these kinds of calls? What could a firm do to help you get through the day? Could they give you a venting session? Could they have yoga in your office? Is there anything that ever comes to mind like, "It would be nice if we had this"?

Hero #3: A treadmill.

Mullins: Why do you say a treadmill?

Hero #3: Well, because I feel that walking on a treadmill for maybe five or 10 minutes kind of calms you down and releases stress. Or just go take a walk. Something that will take your focus out where you can rethink your thoughts, like an area to walk or something like that.

Mullins: You've done a wonderful thing here and we're going to send you a copy of the book.

Hero #3: Oh, outstanding! I hope I was a help to you.

Mullins: You were a very big help, not just to me, but to everybody who's going to read the book.

Hero #3: Thank you so much.

Mullins: Take it easy. Thank you so much.

Hero Update

Just before we went to press, we received this update from Hero #3.

Chris,

I know that being an intake person is not easy, however the reward of helping someone is enough to put a smile on your face.

I just wanted to add one thing more that came to mind. The way an intake specialist sounds on the phone with care and understanding is very important and this will make or break the call. If there's a chance the caller will decide to hire the law firm, then how we sound on the phone is a very important key. People are looking for someone to care, to be heard and understand what they are going through. This will determine if the prospective client will consider hiring our firm.

Regarding your question about what would I do if I were a CEO of a law firm? What would I do to help the intake specialists? I just thought of something real cool, the idea for stress release. A room that has a soft sofa, nice pictures, a waterfall fountain on the wall, a fish tank and maybe some soothing music to ease the stress and some good hot tea.

Chris Mullins Interviews Hero #4

Hero #4: Hi, Chris.

Mullins: Hi, how are you?

Hero #4: I'm good. I'm sorry that I'm calling in late, but I was taking case number 67.

Mullins: It's just you and me.

Hero #4: Okay. This has been a tough month. Every other month, I always count the people below me. I've never made it to 66 up until last month. I would always count and I never wanted to be at the bottom. I always try to stay in the middle. Well, up until today, I was number three.

Mullins: What?

Hero #4: I got kicked out to number three today. Two people moved ahead of me, but I have been in third place all month. I was counting so there are more people below me now, instead of people above me. Too cool, huh?

Mullins: That's awesome. I'm proud of you. I'm getting watery-eyed! So, do you know what this phone call is about?

Hero #4: I'm pretty honored, I heard you're going to interview me. I'm amazed. I don't understand why.

Mullins: We're publishing a book called *Intake Specialists: The Unsung Heroes of Law Firms Worldwide*.

Hero #4: I'm honored. I really am! Like I told you before, if I can help somebody else. All the more power to you Ms. Chris!

Mullins: Alright, are you ready?

Hero #4: I'm ready.

Mullins: Okay, so the questions aren't in any special order and it's off-the-cuff because I want it to be natural.

Hero #4: Okay.

Mullins: How long have you been an intake specialist?

Hero #4: It will be nine months.

Mullins: What did you do before that?

Hero #4: Before that, I was in intake, so we're talking 13 years. Not for a law firm though. I basically did the same thing, I qualified people for disability. But I've been here nine months.

Mullins: So you weren't doing this particular career at the moment?

Hero #4: Correct.

Mullins: Can you remember — you might need to take a moment — one of the most difficult calls you can remember taking? One that was so hard, so heart-wrenching, that you had to keep your cool and stay focused?

Hero #4: Yes, I've had several like that. One was a wounded soldier. If I remember correctly, he was 28 years old. He had disability through the VA, but because they had messed up his records, a lot of what he should have been getting, he was not getting. They were basically saying that he hadn't been in the service for four years. As we started talking and I started gathering information — he had PTSD, he had depression, anxiety — he shared with me that he needed to be able to get this help and that he has been having... hold on, I'm going to cry. He's been having terrible thoughts about suicide.

He shared with me that he had four kids, they were living with his wife's parents because they couldn't afford a home. The little one, I could hear him talking. He was sharing with me how he wasn't getting the right help from the VA. He could not support his family, he's 28 years old and he had been thinking about suicide. He wouldn't tell his wife because she was in the military also and he knew that would scare her.

Mullins: He wouldn't tell his wife?

Hero #4: He wouldn't tell his wife he was having those thoughts because he knew it would scare her.

Mullins: Why wasn't he getting help?

Hero #4: The military had messed up his service stay and were basically only showing that he had been in the service for five months instead of four years. He was not getting the medication or the help he needed.

Mullins: So what did he say to you?

Hero #4: We have a question that asks if you are having suicidal thoughts. When we were talking, he shared that the PTSD and the anxiety was so bad that he wouldn't admit it to his wife, but he was having awful thoughts. Because of my background, I said what do you mean by awful thoughts? I said, "You're not talking about hurting yourself, are you?" And he said, "Well, I have those thoughts." I asked if he meant having suicidal thoughts and he said yes and he said he wouldn't dare tell his wife because she would really worry. So I said, "Do not do that, you just cannot do that! We're going to get you help." I assured him that I would be praying for him and he was not to do that. I don't know how much you want me to say...

Mullins: Just share what happened.

Hero #4: I told him I was going to share something with him. We really connected because he was so young. I really had to get into depth of what was causing him problems because he's still young. You really have to do a very complete interview to show that he really does qualify. He didn't have any backup from the military because his records were so messed up. It really took a long time to make sure I had the documentation, the drugs and everything. But I said to him, "Suicide is a terrible thing to do to the family. Don't do that to your wife and kids, like, I can hear your kids. You just need to hang in there till we get help." And he said what would make you say that? I said that I don't share this with people, but someone in my family committed suicide six years ago. It happened, and I'm still working at getting over it. Don't do that to your family.

Mullins: But it's possible it helped him.

Hero #4: Well, I believe at times these phone calls come in divinely appointed and there is just something in his voice which tells me he needs to know that it would tear his family apart. I told him I'm still trying to move forward and you just don't do that to your family. You have two little kids, they need you, don't do that. It's those calls that make it very hard and you want to really help.

Mullins: But how do you get through the call and then adjust for the next call?

Hero #4: Sometimes I get up and take a walk. That one happened to be the last call of the day. Sometimes you just have to take a walk. Because of what we do, the disability, all day long you're hearing about people who are homeless, you're hearing about people who have mental health issues. I'm hearing about people who don't have family supporting them. I'm hearing about people who are down and out. The world gets very gray during my job.

Mullins: I know.

Hero #4: There are times when you have to literally shake off the... negative's not the right word. I literally have to shake off their energy and take a deep breath. Sometimes I get up and take a walk. I go upstairs, walk around the corner, come back down and then back to the phone. Sometimes you have to focus on something other than the negative because that's all I hear all day long.

I didn't do that very well in the beginning. Even though in my previous job I heard about people's illnesses, problems, can't-walk-to-the-bathroom type of stuff, but this is more. You hear about people who are homeless and the government's not helping them. You just have to be empathetic. I've always had an ability to talk to someone over the phone and be able to build a rapport with them. You just have to be empathetic, be able to build the relationship for the moment and since I've been at this job, you really are helping them. I mean, we're giving them a way that they can get an income, that maybe they can get out of the shelter. I just hang on to that and I go on to the next one.

Mullins: What about when you wake up in the morning, when you're getting ready to get out of bed. When does it start in your mind about the type of calls you might have? Does it start when you get in the office or when your feet touch the floor?

Hero #4: For me, more so when I'm in the car. But I like the fact that I'm helping somebody. My family wonders why I'm doing this, but everyday I get to help somebody. And people are really appreciative that you've taken the time. I mean, you're asking them for their most intimate details about what kind of medication, how sick are they, you're asking them do you have money in a checking account? Are you on food stamps? All those important details. And they're basically telling you their life story. You're making them feel bad because you're talking about all the bad things, otherwise, they wouldn't qualify.

But in the end, you're helping them. You're moving them on to the next step so they can file for disability. You've qualified them, you're giving them help. And that's what keeps me going. I know that's kind of funky and crazy, but that's what I like about this job.

Mullins: So you've told me why you do this, I mean, I'm sure you must have meltdown days when you're like I don't know if I can keep going or do you not?

Hero #4: Well, I do. Most of it is because I'm not making the kind of income like I used to, to be honest with you. The other part is although I'm kind of an introvert, I'm very competitive, so when I wasn't hitting my numbers, that was very depressing to me. There are some days that are hard, but I like the people I work with. I like the support we give each other and I pray a lot. That's what really gets me in here in the morning. I pray to God to give me the right phone calls, to help me make my appointments. Dear angels, bring the right calls to my phone and help me stay focused and do the right things today.

Mullins: That makes a big difference though — praying.

Hero #4: People can call it whatever they want. It's just part of who I am. It really is a gift to be able to sit and do this all day long.

Mullins: Oh, I know, it is a huge gift and my hope with the book is that more people who do this will realize even more what a gift they really are because I don't really think a lot of folks who do this kind of job really give themselves enough credit for what they do. Hopefully this will shine a bright light on them.

Let me ask you a question. If you had the power to do anything that you wanted to do, to create any kind of system or support campaign to all the people who are intake specialist with you, some way to help them get through... Everybody has different ways of dealing with phone calls and unfortunately some individuals are having a tougher time. They need more support and more help. So if you were in charge of your firm and you could put together any kind of program that you wanted to help your team member deal with these phone calls a little bit easier, what would you do?

Hero #4: This is the first law firm that I've worked in and it's very conservative. To a certain degree, you have to be. I mean, you're making 80 to 100 phone calls a day and you're only taking four cases, five cases on a good day. So in a way you have to be focused, but the companionship amongst each other is a big stress-breaker. We're not really encouraged to communicate. Just little things, like if somebody accepted a tough case, we'd throw him chocolate. I don't know if there really has to be big dollars, just little ways to pump people up and let them know that you appreciate how hard they work. In the previous company I worked in, they did really good job at it, they don't do it so good here. Just ways to allow people to go destress. It's hard because you're on the phone, so you wait until the last minute to go to the bathroom.

Making those kind of everyday things easier — way to go, pat on the back, go to their desk and say good morning, shake their hand. Even if there was a corner for when you have a really bad call, you can just go stand in a room, sit on a couch for a minute. We have a really nice break room but I have to go to the car and turn on my Christian station, read my Bible. I guess that's the answer for the previous question you have. I take my lunch hour and I have to unwind and destress and do something totally different. I go where I'm facing the main street so I can see the sun and see the grass because I don't have a window by my side of the desk. Then I can come back and be ready to go for the afternoon. That's what I do.

Mullins: That's what we hope for. For example, I don't know if you have ever heard me talk about this or not, but one of things that I talk a lot about to law firms is our Intake Academy venting lounges.

One of the things that I've been trying to talk to the firms about is creating venting lounges throughout the firm so that if somebody needs to walk away, they can go to the special room. It's pretty, it has the sound of water, maybe some healthy beverages, some lounge chairs and couches, a nice window. And people can go in there and be alone. If somebody else is in there, they can ask that person, do you mind if I vent? And that person might say okay and the person gets to talk, then that's just it, and they walk away.

> So in a way you have to be focused, but the companionship amongst each other is a big stress-breaker.

Hero #4: Right, and until you said it I hadn't really pinpointed why I have to go and get into the car every afternoon. But that's it, that's how I get through it. I started doing that from the very beginning and I really hadn't thought about it. In fact, at one point one of the girls said you never sit and have lunch with us. I said I have to go listen to my music. But you're right, that's how I get through the hard stuff. Once I get in my car in the evening, I'm done.

Mullins: That's good!

Hero #4: Other than this one guy that I've prayed for now, he's on my mirror. That's it. I go home. I'm done. I don't think about my cases. I just turn it off and I prepare myself in the morning to get here, do whatever I have to do, think about where I may need to be, numbers, how many calls, do I need to call anybody from yesterday. The final list that you advised me, Chris, to keep every night, I do that. I stay probably about 10 to 15 minutes longer at night and I make my list and get ready for the day. Then I'm done until I'm ready to come to work in the morning.

Mullins: Well, that's awesome. I think that you're amazing. I feel grateful that I've met you and became your teacher. You're going to get a copy of this book. Everybody we interview that we publish, when the book comes out, we're going to put their name in a raffle and then we'll pull out a name. Whoever we pick out, we're going to donate five hundred dollars to their favorite charity, in their name.

Hero #4: Oh, my goodness. Chris, how fabulous!

Mullins: You get to be a part of that.

Hero #4: Well, I'm the blessed one, honey. You didn't know it, but God put us together at the right time of my life when I was ready to drop my past. Can't drop it totally, but drop to the degree where I can move forward and you helped me do that. I'm very grateful for that.

Mullins: I appreciate that.

Hero #4: Remember, I've been dealing with this for years. Prior to doing phone work for the last 15 years. I was a manager. I worked in a hotel, I did a multiunit supervision. Then 15 years ago, because the pay was good, I went to a call center. I went from walking and talking and motivating people to just sitting there on the computer. It really wasn't me. I stayed with it because it was good money. I had my months where I was on top, you know, I wouldn't have stayed there that long if I hadn't. But I wasn't a continuous top performer. I never was on the bottom, I was always in the middle or slightly above the middle. When my family member committed suicide, there were years that I barely hung on because of the big question that I asked you in our last little private one-on-one training session. Help me get to 66, I don't know what made me ask you that.

Mullins: I know.

Hero #4: That was a miracle. And I can't thank you enough for that. And then I did it twice!

Mullins: I know and we're talking again.

Hero #4: And I'm going to do it. I need a vacation soon. But you can't hit 66 and take a vacation. So I think I'm going to have to work all the way through to make sure I can do it three times.

Mullins: You can do it and I hope that you keep me updated.

Hero #4: Oh, absolutely. You are my first email.

Mullins: That was awesome when I got your email.

Hero #4: Thank you, Chris, I really appreciate it.

Mullins: You keep doing it and we'll give you the book as soon as it comes out.

Hero #4: Okay, great.

Mullins: Just continue to be a bright light.

Hero #4: Thank you, dear. We're studying that at the Bible study I'm doing and I will do my best. I can't believe you came out with that word. That was a divine statement you just made. God bless you, sweety. You take care.

Mullins: Alright, we'll see you soon. Bye now.

Chris Mullins Interviews Hero #5

Mullins: My first question for you is how long have you been an intake specialist where you are?

Hero #5: I've been here about a year and a half.

Mullins: That's it? What did you do prior to this?

Hero #5: I was a store manager at Victoria's Secret. I was in customer service. I majored in political science, but this is my first real job at a law firm.

Mullins: Prior to this, you were at Victoria's Secret and prior to that, you were in school?

Hero #5: Right. I was working at Victoria's Secret while I was in school. I finished school about a year ago.

Mullins: Wow, okay. Can you remember when you took this job why you took it? I hear all kinds of different answers when I ask that question so it doesn't really matter to me, but do you remember why you took it?

Hero #5: I don't remember exactly why. I remember they were telling me about the position and I initially came in for an interview for a paralegal. I'd like to be a case worker and management had said something about my personality, they felt like it would be beneficial to place me in...

Mullins: You'll have to speak up just a little bit, okay?

Hero #5: Okay. I initially interviewed to be a case worker, and management had suggested that I'd be in this position, I guess because of my personality. I was nervous at first when they said that I was going to be talking to people who were recently involved in accidents, or the type of social security clients that I was going to be speaking to. It was really nerve-wracking thinking I wasn't going to be having that much interaction. It was a big difference coming from a customer service position where I was dealing with people face-to-face. So that was a challenge.

Mullins: Tell me about one of those that you can remember, one of the most difficult phone calls that you had to take of where you really had to hold it together. The stories that they were telling were just unheard of and you had to keep it together.

Hero #5: I remember this one client in particular. She was a social security disability client. She had called our law firm because they had stopped her benefits. What happened was she was living in an illegal residence, so they weren't delivering her mail and they stopped her benefits. She wasn't aware of the situation that she was up for requalification or whatever. She's legally blind. Because of her circumstances, even though she is on medical treatment and everything, there was an issue with an overpayment with social security and when these types of cases come up, unfortunately, we can't represent them.

I felt so bad for this lady. She actually went down to the local social security office to request documents from them just stating the amount she owed. Her ex-husband took her, but when she was there at the office, she fainted. Her ex-husband went to go help her and security wasn't aware, I guess, that they were together. So security actually attacked her ex-husband when he went to help her.

Mullins: They attacked him?

Hero #5: Yes. Even after that visit to the social security office, even with the documents she had sent me, we were still unable to help her. She's legally blind, she fainted at the local office. I guess she said that the office was really hot and she was having some trouble. She doesn't really go out much and after all of that happened, we are still unable to help her. That case really stuck with me and that was when I was initially hired, so it was like one of my first cases.

It's just one of those things where you... You hear different cases all the time where people yes, they're technically eligible, but at the same time, they aren't as medically severe as others. When you hear a case like that and since she had other issues on top of that, you just feel so terrible that you can't do anything.

Mullins: I've talked to a lot of folks like you and, as you know, I listen to thousands of recorded real prospect phone calls every month with the permission of the law firms.

Hero #5: Right.

Mullins: Have you ever had any calls where people have said, "Look, I'm going to kill myself?"

Hero #5: Of course, especially with my worker's compensation clients. These are people who have worked their whole lives. They're injured on the job and you hear these stories about clients being terminated. It's overwhelming. The bills keep coming and for whatever reason their spouses a lot of times don't work. Its really hard to hear these people. They're having trouble with their medical treatments, they're terminated from the job, they're not receiving payments. The majority of our cases are anxiety and depression and things like that. They do develop throughout the case, even from the beginning stages. It's so hard to hear these people who have been working and doing everything according to what they think should be done and according to their work conditions — they're injured. You hear about the doctor telling them they're never going to be able to do this type of work again, ever. And they're never going to be able to return. A lot of these people are middle-aged guys with families. Just having to hear their struggles with worrying about feeding their families and trying to provide and worrying about their health at the same time. Unfortunately, it does get to that point sometimes where they'll call you and say they're having those thoughts or they don't really know what else to do. They try to say that they're going to resort to that.

You can hear the things they're saying, their worries and thoughts. You can definitely tell there's something deeper. That's hard as well because you don't really have any place to recommend treatment or anything like that. It's difficult.

Mullins: So when someone says, "Look, I'm thinking about killing myself. I can't take it anymore." I don't know if that's how they say it, but how do you handle that?

Hero #5: I thankfully I haven't had anyone that has said those exact words but you definitely hear about people all the time that want to just give up. With my social security clients, a lot of their ailments are severe anxiety, severe depression and suicidal thoughts. When they tell you that they're in medical facilities for months and months at a time, because they feel like they can't function on their own or they can't be in an environment where they're at risk of harming themselves, you don't really know what to say. Sometimes you don't really know how to comfort them or provide them with hope or faith that things are going to be better. It is hard to try and keep their faith up.

You want them to have confidence in your firm, knowing that you're going to be able to help them or you're going to be able to make things better. It's hard when they're at those low points in their life where they feel like no matter what anyone says or is offering to do, it doesn't feel like it's going to get any better. It's hard trying to establish faith in them or it's hard to get them to try to have faith in you. And that's basically what you have to try to do in every single conversation. You have to try to win their trust and win their faith in the course of a 30-minute phone call.

When they're calling and they're at that stage when they're feeling they would rather die, you have to deal with all of this. It's tough and there are a lot of cases like that.

Mullins: But how do you...

Hero #5: How do I try to remotivate them?

Mullins: I'm worried about you. I'm wanting to know about how do you take care of YOU, one call after the next? How do you regroup?

Hero #5: It's tough sometimes. After you get off a heavy phone call, the last thing you want to do is start over with someone else that has a similar or even worse of a situation. It's tough trying to remotivate yourself, but you try to remember to be thankful. You have a balance between being emotionally involved with the cases but still being professional and making sure that you complete your job up to your environment's standards and everything. I try to constantly remind myself that these are human beings that I'm speaking to. They have real-life situations so I just try to relate to the client as much as possible when we're actually speaking. After that, I sort of use it as a motivator for me to try to help the people who are calling in.

Mullins: Let me ask you this question. Let's pretend, for a second, you have the power at your firm. You have the authority and the power to put together a support program for all the intake specialists at your firm. Everybody who talks to clients and prospective clients, who are over and over again trying to remotivate people, reengage people, help them to feel better, solve their problems, hear the terrible stories.

Email beth@intakeacademy.com or call **(603) 924-1640** to get more information about venting lounges, or go to www.IntakeAcademy.com.

So here you are, you have full authority to put together a support campaign for all of your team members to help them deal with this stress that's not going to go away. Have you ever had ideas or thought about that? You know how it is when you're in the middle of doing your job and every once in awhile, you get this thought and say, if I could do this, this is what I would do, but then you forget it, you lose it, it goes away. What about you?

Hero #5: There are two of us in my department and we try to motivate each other throughout the day and we vent to each other. After we have a rough phone call with a client, we'll just sort of say, "Oh, my God, I feel so bad." We try to vent when we can during the day and tell each other. But at the end of the day, you have to try to put it behind you and recognize that there are other people who need help as well. I use it as a motivator to try and help as many people as I can while I'm here during the day. It is rough, though. There's definitely not a particular way that you handle each call. Each one is so different. There are definitely times where I don't want to continue with the call.

Mullins: Like you want to put out a Do Not Disturb sign.

Hero #5: Exactly. It's definitely hard not to be emotionally involved. I do try to be sympathetic. They are human beings, but when you hear these terrible stories... You feel for them, you understand what they are going through. Unfortunately, with every type of case, everything is very time-consuming, so it's hard to try to keep yourself with it. It's hard to stay present sometimes because you're thinking about everything.

Mullins: Maybe you'll have to think about this and email me later on if you want, it's up to you.

Hero #5: Okay.

Mullins: Here's another thing. What I mean is, for example, I don't know if you've ever heard me talk about this, or if you've read my book in the past or our newsletters. I know when we did your Intake Academy phone sales coaching at your office, one of the things we talked about is I believe strongly that folks who do what you do need to have venting lounges.

Hero #5: Right.

Mullins: Lounges set up throughout different areas of your building that are specifically designed for you to go into to be quiet, to be calm. Maybe there's something like some water running or meditation tapes, positive things on the wall. But no phones, no technology, just a quiet comfortable lounge. A little room that people can go to be quiet with themselves or if somebody else is in there also being quiet, they can ask permission from each other and, with no strings attached, they can vent with no repercussion. Then they walk out and go back to work.

Hero #5: No judgment. Sometimes even when you leave, even outside of work, it affects you. Sometimes when you have a heavy day, you leave, you don't even want to turn on the radio. You don't want to speak to anyone or do anything. You don't want to be social. You just want to go the gym and run for a while or kind of hang out on your own.

Mullins: Or scream, or cry...

Hero #5: Exactly. You have to go home knowing that you have to do it again tomorrow. You really have to be a self-motivator. I feel like you have to have the personality to be able to do it. You have to be able to be connected to someone, even though you're not physically with them. You have to search, within a matter of that phone call, and you have to build that connection. A lot of times it's easy, but sometimes it's tough. When you have an angry client, or someone that is in this situation where they haven't really been helped. They're frustrated, they're angry. There's a lot of different emotions that come with the position that you can't really prepare yourself sometimes.

Mullins: It's absolutely true. And I felt something about you through the various conservations we've had. I think it was in November. I actually told the attorneys at your office. I don't know if they said anything to you or not.

I was on a training class with your team and you got on. There was no internal communication about the class. You somehow found out at the last minute about the class so you jumped through hoops, got your team on the conference call, you were making it happen.

Hero #5: Got everybody.

Mullins: What I learned about you is that you fought to make something happen. Since then I've felt a different kind of connection with you, which is why I chose you.

Hero #5: Oh, thank you. I appreciate that, Chris, I really do.

Mullins: I just want to tell you that I'm proud of you. You make a big difference in everybody's life.

Hero #5: Oh, thank you.

Mullins: I know that things aren't easy. I know that when you work in business, it's like spinning plates. Life happens and you have to kind of just roll with the punches and it's not that easy. I know our Intake Academy phone sales coaching program is not easy. But you got this.

Hero #5: Thank you. We forget sometimes it's a service, it's not even really a business. It's a service that we're providing for these people. It's a lot more personal than a normal job, I guess, would typically be. You develop a relationship with them. Even when they do move on, you still want to help them, even if you can't.

Mullins: Well, my hope and my wish for you is that you continue to be authentic. To do the best that you can, and to always find a way to do better. To not just take care of the call that you're on, but to take better care of yourself. And also see what you can do to help those on your team. You have a gift and I think that you need to step up a little bit more and show your gift.

Hero #5: Okay, I'll try.

Mullins: Share your gift — unconditionally, without being probed — with your team mates, something positive that they did. Work more at being the light with everybody that you approach. Okay?

Hero #5: Okay. Alright. I like that.

Mullins: You can do it.

Hero #5: Thank you.

Mullins: You stand taller and you keep in touch with me and I'll talk to you soon, okay?

Hero #5: Thank you. Have a great day. I'll talk to you soon.

Mullins: Okay, bye now.

Resource: Legal Intake Specialists Association™ (LISA). To learn more, email beth@intakeacademy.com or call (603) 924-1640 and ask for more information.

The five heroes we celebrate in this book will be part of a very special raffle. Intake Academy will put each name into the proverbial "hat" and once the book is published, a name will be selected. This person will have $500 donated by the Intake Academy in their name to their favorite charity. *Congratulations to all our heroes and thank you for what you do — every day!*

Chapter Two

Intake Academy Students Share Their WILs (What I Learned)

What I Learned (WILs)

Read these real WILs from real people who are students of the Chris Mullins' program.

Mallory Beverly at Ricci Law Firm writes, "Don't let the bad calls discourage you. This is more from what happened in the office versus the telephone call, but I think all of this is a learning experience and we need to take the good calls and the bad calls and learn how to improve on these. Even great calls can be made better."

Serena Hernandez at Heard & Smith says she learned that, "I should say the client's name more during the appointment. It makes it more personable and lets them know I don't see them as just another number. I should also acknowledge that they've been on hold for some time and let them know that we haven't forgotten about them."

Lauren Harvey at Schwartzapfel Advocates learned that, "We often talk about the need to sing, check in and express empathy. I like the term best friend voice because if we really pretend we're talking to our best friend, the singing, the checking in and empathy will automatically happen."

Isela Alcalá at Alert Communications says she learned to encourage agents on the things they do right during the calls when giving coaching as well as giving the criticism necessary. She says she will apply this every time she meets with an agent to give them the coaching on their intake calls.

Linda Ramirez at V&B Attorneys says she learned that we should always close with thanking them and telling them that we will be back in touch with them asap whether we can help them or not.

Kevin Sander at McComb Witten says that "each time I attend a session I'm reminded of the importance of making a good first impression. We now have a word for it — zealot."

Christopher Collins at John Foy & Associates says he now fully understands the need for a script. He writes, "I promise to stick to it and provide the best customer service I can. Also, I would like to explain what I meant by unlimited sales opportunities. Each time my phone rings and it's a potential client, I feel confident that I'll not only get the sale, but will also leave a strong impression with the caller. So strong that if he or she is ever considers the use of an attorney, they will only consider John Foy & Associates.

Michael Bastedo at Foy & Associates says he learned that "we need to be assertive and assumptive throughout the conversation. I also learned that we have two sales opportunities in each call. We need to create exact wordage to be used for certain questions involving our attorney fee, and use them daily in role playing. We all also need to follow the script more closely."

Chelsea Vonrhein at Ricci Law Firm says she learned that is okay to ask potential clients the questions on the script even when they seem to be "closed off" because they are the ones calling us. She adds... "The calls that were recorded were not good and definitely made me more aware that improvement is needed. However, I do feel that it would have been beneficial to hear a good call from our office to boost our confidence and to show that the script is being read, then discuss how to improve on that as well. The bad calls need to be addressed but the good calls should also be acknowledged so that we can improve more."

Diana Walker at Heard & Smith says she learned new ways to implement the new script and to gather the necessary information. "I am pretty good with the beginning and the end of the script... and building the relationship. I am going to make a concentrated effort to focus on the wow statement and repeating the crisis statement back to the lead. I am good at catching the crisis statement, but I don't think I repeat it back to them on a regular basis, if at all."

Marissa Anderson at Schwartzapfel Advocates Ltd. says she learned that "we have to strive for that connection with the client with every phone call, even if it takes us off script a little. When we establish a trusting relationship with the client, it can develop a lifelong working relationship. We want them to feel comfortable enough with the first phone call that even if we can't help them, they wouldn't hesitate to recommend us to their loved ones."

Ashley Wilkerson at Hughes & Coleman says she learned how to control an intake, especially if someone who is off topic. And, she writes, "I also learned what IN-T-A-K-E means."

Scott Sellers at Rainwater, Holt & Sexton says he learned the impact and degree that "emotional armor" has on the client/firm relationship. "There is an insight that when speaking with a potential client to show concern and support towards the individual's raw emotion. Not only do these acts of compassion help our firm to stand out, but also creates possible future cases. I am excited to utilize these policies/strategies for future intakes."

Melissa Tingley at Fleschner, Stark, Tanoos & Newlin writes, "In response to our Intake Academy kick-off meeting, I wanted to go ahead and send you my WIL. I did learn a lot during our meeting with Chris. I think one thing that I really took in was about the competition. Often times we get into the mindset that people need our firm, not how much we need them. Also, I had no idea that most potential clients also call three to five competitors. I like the idea that every time the phone rings, the race is on! Another thing that I really enjoyed were the five slats of the Intake Bridge. It really puts into focus what is important for every phone call. While using a script may be difficult to adjust to at first, I think it can only have a positive impact on our department and definitely improve our message consistency. We're all excited to continue working with the Intake Academy and improving our client service along the way!"

Brenda Johnson at Monge & Associates says she learned that "sometimes when we have been doing the same thing for a long time we can tend to sound less empathetic and we need to be aware and check ourselves. We always want to end the call on a call to action. Following the script is key as it has been tested through the span of time. Make sure you are listening to the answers the client gives so as to not miss anything or to ask the same questions over again."

Amanda Salzano at Schwartzapfel Lawyers P.C. learned that every call is important. "We need to be present in the moment when we are on that call. We cannot be annoyed with clients and ignore their calls. When a client gets hostile, ask them to call back or ask them if they want to speak to a supervisor. Quiet rooms or other ways to vent are important. It is normal to be frustrated but you cannot take it on the client. Clients need us and sometimes even when it doesn't seem that way, we need them as well. We can really help a person and be a hero to them. Having a mentality like that makes it easier to do the job. If you are truly miserable day in and day out, you should consider finding a different job. You can get through anything."

Chelsea Donohoe at Geiger Law Office learned that she should focus on keeping her "listening ears" on. She writes, "Clients give us clues into ways we could better accommodate them. I should pay more attention to those clues. I also learned that it is key to get the promise from the client that we will hear back from them if they need to reschedule. It's something that we have been having a problem with in the practice, so it needs to be something I really focus on."

Ariana Tejeda at Marasco and Nesselbush says she learned that we should be glad that the phones are ringing. "We are in a very competitive field and should be happy and grateful that are phones are ringing off the hook. Do a better wow welcome. That helps the client feel more welcome and confident that they called our office. We get to be the heroes for these clients who call Marasco and Nesselbush!"

Candace Floyd at Ricci Law Firm says she learned that it's very important to let the prospect know they have your full attention. "Background noise to them seems much louder than it may seem to us. In the future I plan to address the fact that they have my full attention."

Jessica Del Toro at Berg Injury Lawyers says she learned the importance of client retention. "Not only do we obtain clients through lead generation. The service we provide is what helps us gain the client referrals. The ability to show empathy can help connect with the client to gain their trust. The acronym IN.T.A.K.E will act as a guide to assist our firm and gain financial success and stability."

Liza Salazar-Diaz at the Sawaya Law Firm says she learned how to turn browsers into buyers "in how we communicate with the client, sound concerned and caring about their circumstances. Clients also have a 'five red chair' approach in selecting a firm and we need to be able to seal the deal at the initial contact so the browsers are buyers, and to make sure that the client and I are on the same page throughout the process of the intake call, verifying info and always making sure we try to thank them for contacting us. Build a relationship with them through solid communication and empathy and understanding."

Daniel T. Poli of Schwartzapfel Advocates says, "We never stop marketing ourselves. It doesn't matter if we are advertising on TV, the internet, sitting in a hearing office waiting room, on a train or surrounded by family or friends, there are always clients out there to be had. Whether it be for SSD, WC, BI, or med mal cases, we are in a unique position to become heroes by helping the less fortunate win their cases and providing our clients and their family members with financial and medical benefits — in some instances for life. Those people we help become a source of future referrals knowing the quality of service their loved ones can expect from us. There is always room for personal and professional improvement. What I noticed upon returning to the office in the afternoon was a noticeable increase the level of quality and care with which we handle phone calls for potential clients and existing clients. The impact from the AM session was immediate. We are not just becoming better professionals by sharpening our communication skills, we are becoming better people. That's the difference our clients should feel every time they hang up the phone; that we're not just professionals who are good at their job, we're good people who listen and acknowledge our clients needs, and then ultimately satisfy their needs by winning their case. I would suggest playing back unsatisfactory phone calls on a regular basis to those who are involved, in either a public or in private setting, as it is a very effective method to correct mistakes and ensure they are not repeated. A training session like this was long overdue and I look forward to future sessions."

Ellen Harchut writes, "I just wanted to say thank you for a training class that I thought to be one of the best classes that I've attended on client telephone calls. I took away some great ideas and I look forward to additional training. I learned about how our voice is the most powerful tool with any prospective client and I am going to sound more strong and confident. I need to apply it when speaking with them going forward. I like the opening line 'welcome.' Continually throughout the conversation, keep providing empathy and acknowledgement! Lastly, the closing statement is to be more direct as opposed to saying we will have someone from our intake call you within the next 24 hours."

Melissa Thompson at the Law Office of Shane Smith says she learned to use the three words — grateful, empathy and competition — on a daily basis "to train my attitude while holding a conversation with clients."

John Foy at John Foy & Associates writes, "Today's call was very concerning. My staff needs a lot more training from me. The calls were surprisingly poor. All intake specialists need to follow the script."

Vanessa Ramirez at Heard and Smith says she learned that "Heard & Smith has horrible hold music. But really, though, I learned that I need to slow down and I need to keep reminding myself to be grateful and more empathetic."

Leslie at Charles E. Boyk's law office says that the receptionist needs to "sell the office" and come up with a script.

Amanda at Farah and Farah says not to transfer calls unless they know they're being transferred. "Be knowledgeable and ask the right questions. Get comfortable, focus on one call at a time letting them hear that you're listening. And use their name."

Christina Leggett at Oxner, Thomas and Permar learned that she needs to focus on the bigger picture on why they called (not just for the hours). She says to sound like you care on the phone and make the caller feel like a client.

Maureen Murtaugh at Oxner, Thomas and Permar says to ask more questions of potential and current customers to build a rapport.

Leslie Rombkowski at Charles E. Boyk Law Offices says that the receptionist needs to sell the office and come up with a script.

Pat Misek at the Law Office of Sharon Christie says she'll make sure to have a block of dates/times available at hand so when a prospective client calls, the information is available and time is of the essence. She'll also offer two appointments to the client being careful not to be too pushy or too eager. She adds a personal note... "Chris, many, many thanks for being named student of the month. I do so appreciate this recognition and Sharon is quite pleased with me and your program. We have both learned and attained new skills. Congratulations to you on climbing the mountain — what a thrill. It gives me encouragement to get out and at least walk around the block!"

Leah Mumanus at Cavey & Barrett says to use the name of the caller and repeat the problem/reason why they called. She said she will make the caller feel comfortable and feel like she's really listening to them. She adds that she will answer the phones from now on because it's easy and helps to create a quick and comfortable relationship with a potential client.

Jessica at Farah and Farah law office reminds you to get the contact information, be more sympathetic (show more emotion) and dig, dig, dig more.

Levita Williams at Oxner, Thomas and Permar says she's learned to have a pleasant phone voice, personally welcome the client, be assertive (tell them what you want them to do, don't ask and make sure they know available times), formal language (don't say yeah), use their name in conversation and smile before answering the phone.

Barb Krautheim at Cavey & Barrett reminds you to have sales huddles. Repeat the problem back to the client and share positive things with the staff. She says she is going to try to implement new ideas learned during the monthly calls.

Betty Muir at Walker & Billingsley says she learned it is essential to use telephone scripts. It is essential that the head of the business or manager be involved. It must be an ongoing daily focus and teamwork must be involved. She writes, "You shared two 'horror stories' with us and now I am aware of how customer service should be when I purchase products. If they are not friendly or are curt, I will either make them aware of it in a subtle way or will purchase elsewhere. I worked in customer service for more than 30 years, and I'm not afraid to ask for the manager. I either get good service or I do not give them my business. You felt that it was always important to have them talk to a live person. That is not possible in a law office because we cannot answer questions pertaining to the law or give out any information or advice. Our receptionist is the live person here and she can only make appointments during office hours. It would be too easy for clients to call with questions or problems on weekends and we would not be able to help them."

Shirley Warner at Walker & Billingsley says… "I enjoyed the training session today. I learned 1) to keep the intake call to two minutes or less; 2) to find out the contact information from the caller whether we get the appointment set or not; 3) if we are transferring the call to another staff member, to let that person know who is calling and why so they will not waste time repeating questions. I will use these tools daily at work and encourage others to do the same."

Cara Lyon at Christensen Law Firm says she learned that when speaking to a potential client, the call needs to only last approximately two minutes. Within that time frame we do not use "normal" language, but "absolute" language. This entails: 1) Welcome potential client and get their name; 2) Ask what they are calling in regards to and repeat what they say to make sure you understood it correctly; 3) Ask if you can schedule an appointment to come in and sit down with an attorney; 4) If no appointment is scheduled ask for their contact information so we can mail out our free company newsletter/book; 5) Ask potential client where did you hear about us and, finally; 6) Remember this is similar to a sales call. Sell yourself and the firm. She adds... "I also learned that if you need to put a potential client on hold, say their name and the reason why you are placing them on hold. When you get back on the line with them, tell them thank you for holding and ask how you can assist them. The worst time to put anyone on hold is in the beginning of the call. I will work on applying these steps when answering the phone."

Tara Hirota at Attorneys McComb and Witten's office says that after watching the DVD *Inspecting What You Inspect*... "I found the hearing aid mystery call interesting. I noticed how unsure the employee sounded about the information she was providing. I really think that confidence and training (and yes, a script) would help those taking inbound calls to provide the potential client with the sense that we know what we are talking about. A potential client wants to hire a firm that is experienced and professional. I do not handle inbound client calls, but I do think that 'I'd be happy to help you' will go a long way with any caller and I hope to implement that into my telephone discussions. I also liked the idea of complimenting the client. That is something I can do regularly as I don't deal with prospective clients, but this is applicable for everyone. I must remember to do this when dealing with both co-workers and anyone I speak with on the telephone."

Ed Vega at Cavey & Barrett says to start your day with something positive and share it with your office. Use the name of the caller and repeat the issue.

Vickie at Disparti Law Group says she that when answering the phone to be grateful. "It costs $350 for one prospect. Show emotion, the caller has a problem and they need our help; let the client know they made the right choice by calling us; when passing a call to a caseworker give the caseworker any important info about the client; always be positive and confident when talking to clients and; always use your script."

Erica Lobo at the Law Offices of Bill LaTour says she learned they need to speak to the prospective clients with "love." She writes, "It is not what we are saying to them, it is how we are saying it. Here is how I plan to apply it: by making them feel welcomed to our office and feel the love and by switching up the tone of my voice."

Teresa Wong at Attorneys McComb and Witten's office says the part which most impressed her was the suggestion to place a mirror at her desk. She adds… "I totally agree about the magical effect with the use of the mirror. I will put a mirror at my desk and when I'm being impatient with a troublesome client, I will look at the mirror, see my impatient face and I will shape myself up immediately."

Melissa S. Chavez at Heard and Smith writes, "We were discussing different scenarios on how to keep a client calm and still move forward with claim after the client gets upset about a certain situation. Chris reminded us to pause and listen to the client and let them vent out their frustrations. Specifically we are having problems with a system update we have installed regarding how we complete appointments. We are having problems with a client not being called when we said we would. We need to be reminded we are their 'rock.' She stated to expect those type of phone calls so that when they happen we are better prepared. We need to show the clients 'nothing but love.' She then stated to show them compassionate interest by using phrases like 'the entire team is behind you.' I think this will help during those tense phone calls. Thank you."

Brenda Johnson at Monge & Associates learned that "we must make more effort to make our clients feel comfortable talking to us because it will help build a relationship with them. Showing empathy is important because everyone wants to be understood, showing empathy tells the client we can relate to their situation and that we want to help if it is possible. We should be grateful when the phone rings and consider it job security. It is important to speak slowly and clearly so we can be easily understood. We cannot show empathy unless we listen, allowing our mind to wander or not being there mentally can damage the relationship we are trying to build with the client. Also, it is important to listen because we don't want to keep asking the same questions because we didn't pay attention to their answers that sometimes cover a multiple subjects at one time. Make sure you are responding correctly to the client. We don't want to say 'great' when the client says their doctor took them out of work, because this is devastating to their livelihood and is anything but great. 'I am so sorry you are going through this' is a better and more empathetic thing to say. The WOW opening and closing are important because that is where we either gain or lose our clients. Always make sure the client knows that we are happy that they called. Keep your terminology simple so that you do not talk over the clients' head, this can be very frustrating and can make them feel small when they don't understand. Being empathetic is important, but taking control of the conversation is key, not only because we want to make sure we get accurate information but we want to guide the client to get what we need to make our determination. Control without taking them hostage. Be strong. Explaining the process, discussing fees, what is expected regarding retainers and when we should expect them back will hold them accountable and are important components to completing the intake. This should be done, however, without giving the impression that you are giving legal advice when you are a non attorney."

Christina Moraga at Alert Communications says she learned in class that sometimes you have to come out of your comfort zone to learn and grow, even though it's stressful and embarrassing. "I will try to pull myself out of my comfort zone more often, and do new things with the agents and my team."

Bryan Krueger at Ward Black Law writes, "I enjoyed hearing Annie and how well she did with the caller. I like how she kept control of the conversation without dominating it. I did feel that the call was ended a bit abruptly even though it wasn't really. I like the idea of asking something like 'Is there anything else I can do for you?' or 'Do you have any other questions?' to end the conversation."

Cathy Brann at John Foy & Associates says that since they went over several types of calls she found this training session to be particularly helpful. "You can get a curve ball (call) thrown at you at any time and I can see where the script comes in handy so there is less fumbling, but you have really got to be on top of your game to be able to handle all types of call smoothly and professionally. I learned that a sense of urgency or immediacy is needed and to treat each call as if it were my first. Being pretty new that is not hard. I need to repeat info more often and use their name more during the call. I have no problem with empathy because that comes naturally, sometimes I feel terrible for the caller and have to control my voice. The part where you said to use 'your best friend voice' is a great way to put it. Thanks so much, I am looking forward to the next training session and I am reviewing all scripts and tips as a refresher."

Richard Cassar at Schwartzapfel Lawyers says that "my main takeaway from today's call is to make sure to look after myself by watching my exercise regiment, diet and being mindful to take breaks when needed. I will ensure that I continue to perform to my best abilities. I also need to be mindful to vent my stresses daily either to my coworkers or family to keep my mind clear. From the call today I am grateful for my family and home."

Wendy Stewart at Brooks Law Group writes, "One of the biggest things that stuck out to me today is that 'change is good.' We do tend to become complacent in our comfort zones and if we always do that we will never grow. Thank you for the reminder and encouragement to keep growing."

Christopher Collins at John Foy & Associates learned the importance of customer service and the proper ways to place someone on hold. "It's not a good thing to place anyone on hold for an extended amount of time. If we have to place someone on hold for over 15 seconds we should alert them. And, as always, we must stick to the script. Thanks for the training!"

Mysty Dwyer at Brooks Law Group writes, "I just wanted to say that I got a lot of feedback listening in on this call today. It is nice to hear how other offices utilize their training. I learned a lot during all of the calls, but I will pay more attention to how I may sound to our clients when I am on the phone with them. I do not want them to feel like I am trying to rush them."

Scott Sellers at Rainwater, Holt & Sexton says he learned the impact and degree that "emotional armor" has on the client/firm relationship. "There is an insight that when speaking with a potential client to show concern and support towards the individual's raw emotion. Not only does this act of compassion help our firm to stand out, but it also creates possible future cases. I am excited to utilize these policies/strategies for future intakes."

Annette Box at Heard and Smith After writes, "After speaking with Chris concerning my bad habit of talking over people, she gave me several good hints to retrain myself. The main thing is for me to start my retraining of myself on a personal level and then it will translate to my professional life also. I would never have thought of starting in that area of my life first and will begin that process today. Thank you."

Tracy Sugg at Ricci Law Firm says she that "we have to put more love into our calls. Every time I answer the phone, I will be grateful for the opportunity to have a job, which most of our callers do not have. I will be honest with our callers, sing to them and coax them through the process — each and every call."

Jasmine Rouse at Monge & Associates learned the importance "of how I can personally affect the bottom line by implementing goals for myself and ways to ensure I reach them. I also learned the importance of being a better listener to the client's concerns and/or the specific facts of their case to build a relationship while being externally focused vs. internally focused."

Ariana Tejeda-Harpur at Marasco & Nesselbush says she learned to always ask the what prompted you to call question so we know what is going on emotionally. The receptionist needs to slow down when answering phones so the potential client doesn't feel we are rushed. Always check in with clients during the phone call to make sure they're doing OK. You have to blow clients out of the water because they will be calling three to five other law firms besides Marasco & Nesselbush."

Emily Corwin at VB Attorneys says she learned that "we really need to focus on adhering to the script throughout the call, and that we need to slow down, be empathetic and really make people feel like they've called the perfect firm for them. I'm going to work with everyone to make sure we're putting this into practice. I'm meeting with Brian and Vuk about getting the team to really focus on doing intakes right from start to finish."

Susan Custer at Mallard Law Firm says she learned that there is a $200 minimum marketing expense for each potential client. We need to make the most of the call when they call in. Make sure you always get contact information to send a free book and put in our marketing data base. Your first response should always be empathy. Sound strong and redirect the call and go back to the script. Catch team mates in the office doing something well and compliment them — random compliments."

Chelsea Donohoe at Geiger Law Office says she learned how important the checking in steps are for the client experience. "It really breaks up our somewhat lengthy list of questions and keeps us in control of the conversation. Otherwise, the call can go for much longer than necessary and become frustrating for both us and the client. We also discussed how to stall, which is extremely important in the legal world. We don't want to get into giving legal advice over the phone. When I am doing an intake call, I will keep my script in front of me and really focus on utilizing it as a guide. I will have STALL written on it as well to remind me to always defer the client from asking specific legal questions. The script will also remind me to take quick moments to stop and check in with the client, especially during the intake questions."

Tiffany at Heuser & Heuser writes, "I think the Intake Academy is going to be a great tool for the firm to use. Key aspects: We're all on the same page, we follow the script and sound like the call we're on is all that matters at that moment in time. We put ourselves out there to be the best call out of the 5 the prospects make to other firms. We stay the same from the beginning to the end of their case."

Carrie Hall at Fleschner, Stark, Tanoos, & Newlin says she learned a lot from the Intake Academy. "I like the new introduction saying welcome instead of just hello, and that having a client promise to call you enters them into a verbal contract and will increase the likelihood of further contact between the client and myself. I did not realize there are two types of introductions — reactive and responsive. I can see how being logical and engaging would be more profitable in any aspect. The talk step is the most important key to being a great intake specialist as well as treating each client with love and respect, almost like talking with grandma."

David Carswell at Rainwater, Holt & Sexton says he was impressed by the need "to get the potential client's permission before moving into the talk phase."

Kara York at Hughes & Coleman says she learned to make sure to watch your tone. "Even though you might not realize it, you could sound hateful to the person on the line. Don't forget to show the caller compassion. The phone can pick up more sounds than you realize. Make the call more personal by using the caller's name."

Cecilia Santos at Marasco & Nesselbush says she learned that we still need to work on our wow welcome. "We have the script part of the intake pretty solid, but we need to work on welcoming each client in a more excited tone. This way they know how fortunate we are to be receiving their call because, as you reminded us, it costs us money to get the phones to ring and we want the clients calling in to know we appreciate every one of the calls."

Theresa McLaughlin at Berg Injury Lawyers says she learned that we must make a conscious effort to maintain the mindset that we are helping people and not running a factory. We have to include a bit of emotion and caring into the intake process in order to be successful in obtaining new clients as well as maintaining our previous clients.

Kelly Moderwell at Fetterman & Associates says that it's important to have a script ready in order for the caller to know why your firm is the best choice. Have a sales pitch with adjectives that describes your firm such as 40 years experience with a sound reputation in the community, I have worked for the company for 10 years, our communication network is important to us and you will have access to myself or the attorney within 24 hours during the week. We place a personalized approach to each case and, yes, we have handled many auto accidents for people, but your accident is unique to us because it's yours. When dealing with push back to bypass the intake specialist, divert the conversation back to the caller with, "I have two simple questions to ask you and then I will have an attorney speak with you. Have you been injured and how did it happen?" Always, the relationship first, business second. Who doesn't enjoy talking about themselves?

Karyn Johnson at Brooks Law Group says she has learned the importance of empathy. "I think we do a good job of that here at Brooks Law Group, but it was nice to hear it live, to hear what it sounds like on the receiving end, both useful and less than useful."

Chapter Three

Chris Mullins

"*Every morning in Africa, a gazelle wakes up. It knows it must outrun the fastest lion or it will be killed. Every morning in Africa, a lion wakes up. It knows it must run faster than the slowest gazelle, or it will starve. It doesn't matter whether you're the lion or a gazelle. When the sun comes up, you'd better be running.*" – Christopher McDougall

From this point of Chapter Three forward, you're about to embark on a new sales culture for your entire firm. If staff aren't trained properly on exactly how to handle incoming calls, you'll lose money. Flush it down the proverbial drain, so to speak. And, for that reason alone, you're about to be introduced to the Phone Selling Expert of our time, Chris Mullins. Chris is known by thousands as the Phone Sales Doctor™. She would love to hear your feedback and learn more about you. Feel free to email beth@intakeacademy.com. You'll love working with the Intake Academy and their entire team of In-House Experienced Certified Coaches, and so will your team.

The Evolution Infrastructure of the Receptionist

Receptionists have always been known as the "girls." Still today I hear clients say things like "my girls." If you call them the girls or your girl, that's what you get; the old school gal Friday that will just yes you and do whatever you want, including making the coffee.

What's incredible is in many businesses, especially yours, is you're spending an astronomical amount of money on marketing (for many of you, millions every year) to get your phones to ring with leads, prospects and hyper-responsive clients. They called you now because your marketing is exceptional. You finally figured out the right formula, your marketing and sales letters spoke to them, they did their job, but you forgot about Chris Mullins' Number 1 Rule — Inspect What You Expect™. What happens when the phone rings? What happens to that precious lead? How did the call get handled? Did they schedule an appointment? Or, was the call lost because the receptionist was too busy doing all the other tasks that you require him/her to do? The receptionist has always been dumped on and expected to do all the busy work that other departments can't or won't do. The receptionist is the go-to person for anything that another person in your operation can't get done. It's always been that way; sadly it hasn't changed.

Nothing has changed, really. I see this firsthand with all my clients, not just in the legal niche, but in all types of businesses. Would you, the attorney, be able to deliver a compelling case presentation while at the same time the phone is ringing in your ear and other team members are standing in front of you waiting for you to finish up so they can talk to you? Of course not. You must focus on your presentation, your client communication, your sales skills. This is the same for your receptionist. They must be able to use the Intake Academy Relationship Conversion Script and Intake Screening Questions with 100% focus. This is a skill, an art, and it's not for everyone.

The First Impressions Director's (aka receptionist) job is greet clients and prospects in person with a smile that says don't worry, you made the right decision, you're home now. If you want to keep giving your receptionist all kinds of tasks to do — answer the phone, handle intakes, make call backs, handle email and take care of the laundry — then you'll continue to hemorrhage while turning away prospects and losing current clients and getting no referrals.

You know when you go to a therapist and it's just you and the therapist in the private office and you're not quite sure yet if he gets you, knows you, understands you? You're still testing (interviewing) every moment in your relationship, hoping that this is the one and you can stop the madness of hunting for another, and then... *the therapist looks at the clock!* All it took was that one moment for you to write him off, to feel like he didn't understand a word that you said, just like everyone else. That's exactly what happens to your prospects when they finally decide that NOW, today, this moment is the time to call you, to do the deal with YOU. But you're just not focused on them at that moment, you're mentally somewhere else. You have people standing around you waiting for you to get off the phone. You're short staffed, the phones are ringing off the hook and your intake manager is yelling, "We need people on the phone!" It's not possible to give your all, to become an expert, to win the client, to get that first date with the hopes of marriage if you're not there with them and you're focusing on other things, tasks and deadlines. You must be given permission to focus on that call, at that time, that story, that person and nothing else. You can't do this if you're a Jack-of-all-trades.

First and foremost, do your homework. Take a look at your current operation. Why can't the receptionist do it all? What's getting in the way? Do you have other team members on board that could help with call volume when the receptionist is on the phone? Do you need to hire more staff to handle the incoming calls? Before you jump to make any changes in your staff, examine your current situation. How many calls do you get daily? How many of those calls are opportunity calls? How many opportunity calls schedule appointments? How many appointments show up? What happens to the ones that don't show up? What happens to the ones that do show up? What gets measured gets done. What you focus on expands. Know your numbers.

Teach your entire team as it relates to them to know the numbers. Then, if you've determined that you just don't have enough team members to stop the hemorrhaging, here are my expert recommendations in this order:

1) Do not use the First Impressions Director (receptionist) for closing sales on any level. Stop it!

2) Hire Intake Academy Sales Experts to handle all incoming leads. Real salespeople understand the importance of sales, closing, relationships, communication skills, empathy. They love scripts and don't want to sound scripted, they live for their goals and are very competitive, they understand metrics, they understand the bottom line, they understand you have two sales opportunities with all prospective client leads. Sales Opportunity #1 — close the deal; Sales Opportunity #2 — verify all contact information so the firm can keep that prospect in the marketing funnel so it's not a 100% lost lead. When the prospect is ready or wants to refer a friend or family member, they won't forget you. Real salespeople understand to never hang up without either #1 or #2. Real Intake Academy sales experts understand that they're doing a disservice to prospects if they don't have #1 or #2 secured, because now what they've really done is left the door wide open for those prospects to run to your competition.

3) Hire more sales experts to handle the incoming leads.

4) Create your own internal on-site call center even if you're only starting with a few people.

5) All prospect calls get directed to this team.

6) They are the closers. It's their job to close as many appointments as possible.

7) Give them a sales goal and hold them accountable for it.

8) One of Chris Mullins Famous Formulas is called RMFD — Record, Monitor, Feedback, Daily. Record the calls (check laws for recording calls in your state).

9) Monitor: Listen to the recordings.

10) Feedback: Share the recordings with the team.

11) Daily: Give healthy constructive criticism (no abuse, yelling, swearing, throwing things) *after* the team, especially the person whose call you're listening to, critiques their own call.

12) Criticism with love: "Mary, here's what worked on your call. It was incredible. Keep doing it. Here's what the opportunities are, here's why it needs to be fixed and here's how to fix it."

Managing partners, CEOs, COOs, marketing directors, you're not alone. You can do this. One step at a time. The Chris Mullins Phone Sales Doctor™ and in-house team of Intake Academy coaches work with law firms on how to set up their own internal call center, how to set up their own internal Intake Academy phone sales training and how to get their team to do what they want them to do. We Inspect What You Expect™.

You're also putting too much stress on your receptionist and your entire team when you don't have a dedicated sales team, which I also call your insurance policy for marketing dollars. Do you really want team members who are white-knuckled all day long, heart beating fast, stressed out, afraid of making mistakes? They don't want to come to work, they go home and talk about how terrible their job is at the dinner table with their family? No, I don't think so. Think about the time, money, energy and effort you put into marketing campaigns. How much time, money, energy and effort do you put into your team?

Let's assume that you have the right people on your team. Invest in them, support them, coach them. You, the owner, are the most important person to your staff. They want to do good. They want to help you. They don't want to let you down. Be there for them.

The Number One Job

You're not in the legal business as much as you're in the relationship and healing business. Most of you are spending an astronomical amount of money every month to get your phone to ring with prospective clients, to get prospects to ask questions via your web site using

> **Resource:** To learn more about the Intake Academy Intake Sales Specialist Hiring System, email beth@intakeacademy.com and ask for more information.

your web chat service and paying huge amounts to outside lead agencies to send you leads that your team now has to learn to do outbound sales calls. You're winning because your phones ARE ringing which means you finally figured out the perfect formula to get the right type of prospective client to call you. They've raised their hand, they've pre-qualified themselves based on your marketing message. You spoke to them, they said hey, that's me, they get me, they know me, I'm going to call them now because it's time, I'm ready.

Perhaps you're spending a minimum average of $500 just to get one prospective client to call you. The intake specialist's *number one job* is to close the deal. This is, of course, assuming that you're sending prospective client calls to the receptionist. To take that prospect and turn them into a sale, an appointment, a client — *that's it*. It's impossible to have the person taking your incoming prospect calls and turn them into clients if they have to also worry about the list of other tasks you've given them: greeting clients as they come into your office, making outbound calls, scanning reminder calls, setting up the conference room for a meeting, billing, etc.

Once they hear that phone ring everything has to STOP. Nothing else matters. Only that call and the desired outcome, which is always one of two things: close the appointment or get the complete contact information. You cannot be an expert at everything. As soon as you, the owner/attorney, gets this and embraces this, everything will change for your firm. The intake specialist (receptionist) must be in a state of readiness always.

Shocking Facts!

Most business relationships rely on the telephone, and how you sound makes up 84% of the message you send. When a prospect or client decides to finally get around to calling you because of the promotion you sent them in the mail, they want to talk to you, the live person!

Your answering machines or voice mail can't sell them, or in the first few minutes say, "Wow, you called the right place!"

More Shocking Facts

Eighty percent of *new* clients will not call back or leave a message when they get a voice mail or answering machine. Only 25% of business owners even believe the telephone has a major impact on their business (even though it is the only point of entry for all new clients).

Some Statistics

Smile   *The science of smiling. What happens to our brain when we smile?*

Let's say you experience a positive situation and you see a friend you haven't met in a long time. This means that neuronal signals travel from the cortex of your brain to the brainstem (the oldest part of our brains). From there, the cranial muscle carries the signal further towards the smiling muscles in your face. Sounds simple enough right?

And yet, that's only where it starts. Once the smiling muscles in our face contract, there is a positive feedback loop that now goes back to the brain and reinforces our feeling of joy. To put it more succinctly, "Smiling stimulates our brain's reward mechanisms in a way that even chocolate, a well-regarded pleasure inducer, cannot match."

Smiling then, seems to give us the same happiness that exercising induces in terms of how our brain responds. In short: Our brain feels good and tells us to smile, we smile and tell our brain it feels good and so forth. That's why in a recent research study scientists concluded "that smiling can be as stimulating as receiving up to 16,000 Pounds Sterling in cash."

Source: Dr. Niedenthal

Effective Communication

Many people think that communicating effectively is merely a matter of finding and using the right magic words. They believe that using certain words in the right order will get the results they want.

Scientific research tells us that attempting to persuade by words alone is about as effective as trying to chop down a tree with a Swiss army knife.

To be a truly effective communicator, your body language and tone of voice must be consistent with your content. Even the most powerful words spoken in a monotone with lifeless body language will fail to rouse anyone. In a study conducted at UCLA, Dr. Albert Mehrabian found that when verbal, vocal and visual signals are inconsistent, content counts for a mere 7% of the overall message. In such a situation, 55% of the message is transmitted by facial expression and body language; and 38% comes from voice quality — pitch, tone, volume and inflection.

So, when you think about it: If you've been given the luxury of "face time" with a person you want to influence, a warm, friendly smile, a firm handshake and good eye contact can work wonders. But if anything about your voice is flat or distracting, annoying or boring, you've reduced your effectiveness by 38%.

And how often do we spend face-to-face time with our clients these days of phone-computer-fax? Discounting the attractive physical impression, what counts is not only what you say, but how you say it.

Keep in mind when reading statistics like this that answering machines and voice mail to capture new leads from prospective new clients can't possibly convey the message that you're here for them, that you want their business and that they absolutely called the right place, so come in for the appointment.

You've already purchased a phone system. That money is spent. You've already hired staff. Most business owners currently advertise in the yellow pages, newspapers or special direct marketing programs of some kind. The primary goal for all of this spending is to get new clients and they all come through the telephone!

Do you know how many new clients you lost this month? The smarter question to ask yourself is, what do we have to do to fix this problem immediately?

You'll get more ideas when you think like that verses "our business is different." Unfortunately, we sometimes need to use voice mail. Another question is how much are you spending each month on marketing to get your phone to ring? That alone should be enough reason to say we need to take what we're uncovering with our phones in our business to fill the holes in our bucket, fast!

We need live people on the phone to give every new prospective client what they want — a live person — so let's provide a solution and test a few ideas to see what works best.

How do you know that the messages you are getting are being captured? Don't put this off. There are few concerns more pressing than this one, because every new lead, every referral, every single dollar that you spend on advertising is driving new clients to one place — your telephone. All the phone training in the world won't help your staff to set new appointments if they don't answer the telephone when the call comes in.

We would all like to think that new clients would conveniently leave their name and number when they get your voice mail, but the fact is it rarely happens. Existing clients and people trying to give you money might leave a message (they won't like it), but a brand new client will most likely call somewhere else.

When they finally tip over to make that call, they're ready to talk to you — a LIVE person. You've got to be ready to say, "You've called the right place. I have an opening today at 10:00."

When someone calls you after business hours, they are not really expecting you to be there. When they call at night, they were planning to leave a voice mail. On the other hand, when they call during business hours, they are expecting to reach you.

Stop the Hemorrhaging

So, for many clients, they're conditioned, and therefore expect, to reach you during 8:30 am until about 6:00 pm. These hours must be covered by a live person. Do you know how many hours per week your phones aren't covered by a live person?

What about the prospective clients who call your business during lunch break? Are you answering the phones during those times?

Businesses that use their telephones for the main point of entry to their business must focus on their telephone expertise just as much as they do with the technical aspects of what they do and the time and money they put into lead generation marketing.

Even More Shocking Facts

Here are 14 top excuses why your phone isn't being answered by a live person. Here's what we (the Intake Academy team) hear from students and members (your staff) across the country and worldwide on why they couldn't get to the phone and/or why it went to voice mail.

1) I was with a client, no one else picked it up. I'm only one person.

2) I'm exhausted. I put my phone on do not disturb and put my head down.

3) I'm trying to a hire a new intake specialist to answer the phone and schedule appointments. I can't hire someone until I get the go-ahead from the attorneys. That was four days ago, now, I have an open house to attract new clients but no one to help with the phone to make appointments and give directions for the open house.

4) I was in the back taking a break, didn't hear the phone.

5) I had a doctor's appointment. The person who's scheduled to help me didn't show up yet, but I had to go.

6) Everyone is busy with other clients.

7) We don't have call forwarding.

8) I'm new and just thought someone else would pick it up.
9) I had the day off.
10) I couldn't get into work because my car wouldn't start.
11) I got a call from the daycare and needed to pick up my daughter.
12) I had to have lunch, it's my time, if I don't take it I don't eat.
13) I didn't know how to take the phone off our outside answering service or answering machine.
14) We don't have voice mail. If I'm on the phone and someone else calls, my phone beeps, but sometimes it's hard to take that call because I'm already concentrating on the person I'm speaking to, so hopefully they'll call back.

Arghhh! Stop Putting Callers on Hold

Especially before you even meet them, greet them, get their name or know why they're calling, I personally call clients to check in on their phone skills. One day I was on hold for three minutes with a client. Please, this is not acceptable!

Stop the Hemorrhaging

Don't you feel that way as a consumer? Doesn't it tick you off when it happens to you? Fix it! That doesn't mean, "Chris, we've always done it that way or we have no one else," etc. It means you're losing hundreds or thousands of dollars. Let's step way out of our comfort zone and decide to fix it. Then, and only then, will you come up with tons of solutions you never thought of before.

Eight Instant Stress Busters in 20 Minutes for the Intake Specialist, Receptionist and the Front Desk
Source: Lonny Brown

Even in the middle of a stressful day, you'll fair better using a few strategic destressing exercises. These real-time coping skills comprise a holistic progression from body to mind to spirit. Choose the best ones for the moment, or complete the whole routine within 20 minutes.

Stretch: Feel better immediately — without even getting out of your chair — by slowly bending forward, leaning back and twisting your spine in both directions. Standing, slowly reach for the ceiling inhaling, then bend and reach for your toes, exhaling.

Progressive Muscle Flex/Release: Tense strongly from feet up, and hands inward, while inhaling through the nostrils. Release suddenly, from head to toes, exhaling through the mouth.

Self-massage: For stimulation and relaxation, rigorously massage your head, neck, face, hands and feet.

Eye Palming: Rub your hands together vigorously until hot; place them over your closed eyes for soothing energy.

Breathe: Squeeze all air out from the belly up, then inhale, fully expanding abdomen, rib cage and upper body. Pump the breath in and out forcefully from the belly to stimulate internal glands and organs. Feel the breath passively without controlling it.

Relax: Elicit your "relaxation response" by silently or audibly repeating a word, sound or prayer, ignoring all other thoughts. This internal focus alone can reduce muscle tension, blood pressure and anxiety. Focused mind exercises produce body results!

Balance: Lean forward and back, then side-to-side, reducing movement until still and balanced. Center your awareness deep within the belly.

Get Grounded: Feel your connection to the earth.

Autogenetic programming: Repeat these positive statements in first person, present tense:

- My forehead feels cool
- My limbs feel heavy and warm
- My heartbeat feels slow and quiet
- I feel completely relaxed

The Mirror Technique

Many of you have heard me talk about using a mirror at your desk to remind yourself to SMILE before you pick up the phone, to stay focused on taking care of each call like it was the first one of the day, to shake off any bad experiences you might have just had before the telephone rang.

Read About How Salesmen Quadrupled Their Income During the "Depression Days"

In my old organization, where we had to make a complete about-face to avert disaster, I first used this technique by placing a mirror in a back room of the offices where the employees left their hats and coats. It was placed so that everyone had to see it when entering or leaving the room. At first I pasted strips of paper with slogans such as "We're going to win," "Nothing is impossible to an indefatigable mind," "We've got the guts, let's prove it," "Let's show them we're not licked and then go to town," "How many are you going to sell today?" Later we took soap to write the slogans directly on the face of the mirror.

> How far will you go? Will you put mirrors up in your own business and explain to your team what the mirror technique is all about?

Every morning a new slogan appeared with the sole purpose of convincing our employees that they could get business even though others were struggling to keep their doors open. Eventually mirrors were also placed alongside the door frame of the main door to the office so it was the last thing salesmen saw as they left and more alongside calendar frames on the desks of all salesmen and executives. The startling thing about it was that during the worst of the "depression" days, all the salesmen quadrupled their income.

Ray Kroc famously correctly identified clean bathrooms at McDonald's as marketing. Walt Disney said the same about clean streets at Disney.

This holds true for the telephone! The telephone is the key to your business the first point of entrance (voice) in your business. The telephone will make the business owner look good or bad.

Expert Advice — Dialing for Dollars

Outbound Calls

Does this sound like you when you're calling your clients for any reason at all? Sometimes salespeople will make calls because they're supposed to, not because they want to. They have a negative attitude and a feeling of "I'm just trying to get this done and out of my hair," and the client or prospect can sense it. They're just going through the motions with no enthusiasm.

If they're professional salespeople (which is the mindset you want), they'll have financial goals and should know the exact value of their time and the value of a new client. They need to ask themselves, "If this is the value of a new client, why do I have a bad attitude when I call them on the phone?"

Ask yourself why you're calling clients in the first place. Know why you're calling them, have a script to keep you on track, practice your presentation and believe in what you're doing. If you can't sell yourself on why you're making a phone call, you can't sell them.

Know what your strengths and weaknesses are when you're talking on the telephone. If you tend to get nervous, practice and learn to relax. Practice a script and record it so you can listen to it over and over again. Then listen for where you can pause, take a breath or just relax. Call a friend and role-play over the phone.

Build your self-confidence. Know your business, services and products backwards and forwards. Learn all you can about the marketplace and your clients. The more you know, the more reasons you have to call and the more you can offer, simply because you know more.

When you talk to clients on the phone, concentrate on painting a visual picture for them. You want them to be able to see what you're selling through your words. If you really know what you're talking about and are comfortable selling over the phone, your words take on visual meaning.

Build and/or enhance a relationship over the phone. Call with information important to your client, share something personal or just wish them a happy birthday. Clients will pay a premium for your product or service if they know, like and trust you, and a phone call can reinforce that relationship.

Listen for what the clients' real wants are — really listen. Ask them to repeat something if you don't completely understand what they're saying. It pays dividends.

Know exactly what you want to accomplish from your phone call and get a "call to action."

The Missing Link to Attracting More Clients Uncovered!

Q: Do you know what the missing link is to attracting new clients and referrals to your business?
A: The telephone.

Q: Do you know what the most valuable asset is in your business?
A: Your clients.

In a study conducted at UCLA, Dr. Albert Mehrabian found that talking on the telephone, the actual words you use, account for only 16% of the way you and the products and services you represent are perceived.

The remaining 84% of your impression depends on the sound of your voice and the feelings people get when listening to you. This is important... How do you know when people are ready to buy right now? You don't! You've got to stay in front of them with effective marketing. What happens if you have awesome marketing but your telephone skills are poor? Answer: No new clients.

In addition to effective marketing you've got to make sure that when the phone rings you have top notch professionals answering the phone, ready to close new client appointments and referrals.

Let's say you want just 20 new clients each month. All your marketing is done so that the phone rings with new client opportunities and referrals. What? You think that referrals aren't in the same category as new clients? Not so. Just because they've been referred to you doesn't mean they'll give you their money. It doesn't even guarantee that they'll call, but when they do, you've got to be ready.

Back to the Phone

Your marketing is now working and the phone rings with lots of new client opportunities. That's great, but it's not enough. It's time to focus on your staff; everyone that answers the telephone. Get them excited about the phone each time they hear it ring. Get them motivated and looking forward to closing new client appointments.

Coach your entire team — intake specialists, receptionists, attorneys, case managers, etc. — to think about each case, each prospect as a person, an individual, by name. Talk about your clients and prospects by name with your team, bring them to life. Many firms just refer to their prospects as PCs (prospective clients), but it's critically important that you, the leaders, teach your team to think of all your prospects and clients as people you're helping. Focus on the real emotional pain that you identified during your conversations.

Be sure they understand what sales is, how to answer objections, how to use a script without sounding like they are, how to close referral appointments, how to listen and how to follow up. You can't go wrong with coaching your entire team on telephone skills, sales and customer service relationship marketing.

A long time ago I heard my mentor Dan Kennedy say, "Sales are made everyday. Some will close — you or them. What's it going to be?" Nothing ever happens in this world until someone sells something.

> **Resource:** Sales are made everyday. Someone will close — you or them. What's it going to be?

Ghost Calling

The easiest, least expensive way to organize your incoming client and prospect calls is to set up a marketing phone tracker system. This is a web-based, automated, no-equipment-necessary system. Chris Mullins, along with the Intake Academy (www.IntakeAcademy.com), provides this turnkey phone tracker recording system. The phone tracker system should be used for all your lead generation campaigns. All you have to do is publish your phone tracker numbers in your marketing campaigns that you've created for prospects. You can have a different number for your TV ads, radio, print, direct mail, etc. That way you know which phone number goes with which campaign and you can easily measure if the dollars you're spending on marketing for that particular campaign are giving you a good ROI.

Publish, market, advertise and teach your established clients to call your main phone number so the receptionist at your firm gets all the established client calls. They all ring to her/him; therefore this person is trained on how to handle established clients utilizing a special script, special training because these, too, are sales calls. And all the prospects call a different number and those calls are pointed to a different person or group of people to handle those calls. These folks focus on only prospect calls and they get special ongoing training for that. They get scripts, you monitor calls and give feedback. Be sure to check the laws for your state with regards to recording calls.

Once a prospect becomes a client they get special client-only phone numbers to call to get the fastest service. Train your clients on your voice mail, your conversations, your business cards, your emails, your advertising the number you want them to call and the number you want prospects to call.

Stop the Bleeding! Businesses Are Bleeding

"The bleeding always stops." — Anonymous surgeon

Businesses are bleeding... The way to stop the bleeding is to clamp it off. Here's how we go about it.

As consumers grow ever more disgruntled with customer service, America's retail stores, law firms, restaurants and airlines are investing serious time and money to keep their employees on their toes. Their secret weapon: instant feedback from an army of undercover shoppers.

The best way to avoid call reluctance and lost client sales opportunities is to monitor your staff daily, record their calls and play them back for all to learn. Of course, you also need to give them individual feedback. As always, check the laws in your state regarding recording calls.

How to Break the News to Your Staff

You're probably wondering what that's all about. I'll tell you shortly, but first, here's how you can make the most of my advice.

I want to remind you about the art of translation. The idea is for you to be in the habit, have the behavior, of asking yourself every time you enter an educational moment, read a book, attend a mastermind class, listen to a CD, opt-in at www.IntakeAcademy.com to learn from our FREE coaching videos, opt-in at www.GreatBottomLine.com to get Chris Mullins' famous, free Monday morning email stimulators or even observe others. How can I take what I've just read, heard, observed and apply it to my own situation? I guarantee that you can if you're adept at translation.

I suggest you have pad of paper and pen ready to go. Draw a line down the middle of your page. At the top of one of the columns write in big letters the words SIDE NOTES. This is a strategy I teach students whenever they're in a learning moment. You know, when you're in a seminar or reading a book, attending a meeting or even listening to CDs and suddenly you hear something that excites you. Those are what I call side notes. Write down those items that excite you because those are probably the actions you'll be able to execute right away.

Let's assume for simplicity's sake we all have the right people in place. You need to understand that how your team reacts to "breaking the news" regarding how they handle the telephone is critically important to the success of your message to them. Your mindset is key — you, the attorney, the CEO or COO and your office manager.

Here's what I'm finding on a regular basis when working with clients: The business doesn't have a consistent system in place for how to use the phone for inbound sales opportunity calls.

Or, they had a system, but they don't follow it, or they had weekly Sales Drills™ but got away from it, or had incentives but not any more, or they had a phone script but don't use it anymore — you get the idea. It's up to you. Your team will follow you, you're the one that they want to impress the most.

They also watch you and follow you. So, if you're burnt out, they're burnt out; if you're sloppy they are; if you're not systemized they're not; if you're late or making excuses, they know and will do the same! Resentment is eminent. And if your attitude is,

> "When the student is ready, the teacher will come." – unknown

"Hey, I'm paying the salary, I can do what I want," they'll get that message, too. The message is, it starts with you and your mindset, how you feel about yourself, your business and your future wealth. And it all connects to the telephone! You must make your phone, your sales efforts and your customer service (internally and externally) extremely important. Systemize and stick to it. Your team will follow. I guarantee it!

Never give up. It takes time; it's an ongoing building process. Creating new behaviors is about making decisions, then dumping old habits to make room for new ones. Everything you do in your business with your staff must be from a positive standpoint.

The educational portion of your business, the ongoing coaching and training you're providing for your staff has got to be based on relationships, communication and sales. How you treat your internal customers (your team) is how your team will treat your external customers.

So, when you tell your folks that you'll be doing mystery calling, or ghost calls as we call them in our phone sales program, they won't like it. They'll initially be concerned, afraid, threatened or feel like you don't trust them and that you want to catch them doing something wrong so you can get rid of them or lecture them. (Be sure to check the laws in your state regarding recording calls.)

This is normal and you should expect it. However, if you've been focusing on your own mindset with your business in all the areas I mentioned earlier, it will be easier for them because of the success culture you've created. They'll still be uncomfortable, but it will be a little easier.

Don't back off or get nervous, remember, this is your business, you make the decisions. You've got to monitor your staff daily, you've got to track your incoming calls with the telephone and your outbound sales calls as well. The telephone is the single most important sales and marketing campaign in your business for prospects, clients and referrals in your business. Without the phone and good staff, in that order, you've got nothing! No matter how good you are, you're done.

Ease into this process, explain to your staff that this is a positive program to help them become sharper than ever, to do even better than they already are. To enhance what they're already doing right.

Notice what I just said: better than they already are doing. That's a better message than, "we want to fix what you're doing wrong" or "we want to correct your mistakes."

Now that you've been having checkup calls done, you want to share the news with your team. So...

1) Calm down.

2) Breathe and relax.

3) Remember your purpose (which is to be able to influence your team to repeat the great things they already do and quickly tweak the areas that need improvement. Notice the language I'm using.)

4) Have a plan before you talk to them about their critiques. Take the time to listen to the call recordings yourself and make notes about the good ones first and why it's important for them to continue those good points. Then share. Many folks don't even realize the good they're doing while talking to clients; it's part of their routine, so point it out, that way they can do more of it.

5) Next, share the specific areas that need fixing — give examples.

6) Share why it needs to be fixed.

7) Make sure that you also offer the solution, how to fix what needs fixing.

8) Make this time fun — smile! — you want your team to look forward to your critiques and even ask for them. Believe me they will, this has been my experience.

9) Hold your team accountable for using their Intake Academy Relationship Conversion script, which you need to make sure you have in place.

10) Teach your team how to use the script, practice and reward them.
11) Before you talk with them, you need to know what you want to fix. Put together a lesson plan for how they can fix it, include how you'll help them and when you'll meet again.
12) Commit to your weekly sales drills, listen to calls every week as a group critique together — no excuses.
13) No one likes to hear their own voice being recorded. I personally don't like to listen to my voice, but I do it so I can always be focused on improving. When I was doing public speaking, I was constantly recording my business talks and playing them back.
14) Remember, be sensitive. You're dealing with people, fears, rejection and self-confidence. You need to work at building them up, not tearing them down.
15) Systemize this process.
16) Teach your team to self-critique.
17) Pay attention to them, guide them, coach them, encourage them to visit with you, watch your tone, your words, your body language. Remember, you're always being observed.
18) Make it important, which means you won't drop the ball. Keep at it, because they're waiting for you to drop the ball since it's likely you have done so in the past with great ideas that have gotten you fired up. Not this time though. First you need to build the trust with your staff, even if you've been at this for 20 years. Second, your telephone and your staff are critically important to you, without them you have no business!
19) Give your staff the tools: ongoing coaching, sales training, relationship and communication training, scripts, outlines, FAQs, objections lists with the correct answers, role-play, provide coaching and support for them.
20) Peer recognition — encourage this, require it and systemize the process.
21) Catch your team doing something right, daily.
22) If you're thinking, "Chris, they should know how to do it by now..." that's the wrong attitude. They're people, we need to be continually reminded of what to do and how to do it. And, you need to be sure that you've given them the right tools, guidance, information, training and ongoing coaching and mentoring. It's

just as important for your staff, your business and your bottom line as it is for you!

23) I can guarantee you if you don't handle this moment, breaking the news the right way, sabotage will absolutely show its ugly head with many of your team members.

24) Remember to create an ongoing reward program and recognize your staff, each team member, for even for the smallest improvements.

25) Here's an example of how your introduction can go. It may sound something like this: "Great news! We're going to have the Intake Academy experts, real intake sales specialists, come in to help you and me perfect our phone skills, sales and customer service to improve our bottom line, the number of new client appointments we secure and deals we close!"

Your Business' Most Important Tool

Remember, our telephone is the one tool that opens or closes the door to the business. It must be done well.

Why? Nothing else matters if our phone is not answered well.

Handled well means prospective clients call to schedule and keep their appointments. Established clients keep their appointments.

The first voice that the client hears impacts how we are thought of. If the gate is closed, no marketing will open it.

And if that gate is closed on day one, it is unlikely you can reopen it for the client that just hung up without making an appointment or giving you their information. A closed gate means money is needlessly wasted on follow-up mailings and external marketing.

What to Do With Our Phones?

Measure. That which we measure can improve. How do we measure?

1) Keep a phone log.
2) Record phone calls for critiques at team meetings for training and quality assurance. (Remember to check the laws regarding recording in your state.)
3) Review your recordings and critiques from your Intake Academy coaching portal.
4) Talk about the recordings with the staff and how to improve each one.

The Phone Log at Its Basic

Tons of technology to use these days, many web-based, but if for some reason you don't want to get into any type of technology, just begin with pen and paper. Write down every call. Record the date, time, name of caller, caller's contact information, staff member who took the call, results and dates for any followups.

At your staff meetings (weekly sales drill), look at the log to see what's happening and who's calling your business. Use the log to identify questions and answers that the team must have ready. It can help identify scripts needed for review before answering the phone.

Some clients have such high fear that it will prevent them from showing up even after the appointment is made. We need to detect if a person is fearful and have the right script to handle these people. Without identifying your clients, share stories of other clients in similar situations.

There are questions that occur in a client's mind when they call. (There are also questions that a person might not tell you.) We have to answer the questions in a way that tells the client, "you have chosen the right place, you can feel good about your decision. We have handled people in situations just like yours and you will receive the highest level of quality, care, skill and judgement." A client needs to feel good about making the appointment and looking forward to their visit.

Mystery Shopping! Ghost Calls! Customer Service IS Sales

I read an article in *USA Today* about how hotels are trying to make your stay more personal. They hope you come back again and again.

I thought you might enjoy this list, but I do have an assignment for you involving the art of translation, which many of you have heard me talk about. Get your pad of paper and your highlighter out and make a list of the ideas you really like. Next to each one write how you can translate the same idea into your own business, then pick one and decide on a date to execute it.

Marketing + Incoming Calls + Ongoing Phone Sales Training + Ongoing Monitoring Calls + Daily Goals + Tracking Incoming Calls + Sales Talk (talking about the numbers) + Recognition = APPOINTMENTS = SALES.

With competition keen these days, managers are making it their business to get to know their guests on a personal basis. They know

that special attention keeps them coming back. For instance:
- Hotel bartenders serving your favorite drink before you ask
- Special water, blue chips and blue cheese dip that you like
- A soothing CD in your room after a very stressful day
- Handwritten notes welcoming you back
- How about as you rush in from a rain storm you find your favorite water with the note, "It turned a bad day into a good one."
- Housekeepers notice favorite toothpastes
- Doormen pay attention to where and when travelers go

All the information gets entered into your profile database system. Of course, strategies like this should be used for regular and infrequent guests to keep them coming back for more!

All of these ideas are great and will certainly add value to the experience your clients get, but you still must inspect what you expect even with ideas like this. How do you know it's being done the way it should be done? You don't unless you do on-site mystery shopping and mystery shopping by phone calls. Mystery shopping is simply a quality control training tool, support for your team. That's the message you want to give them, otherwise it will be viewed as if you're trying to catch them doing something wrong.

12 Big Things That Go Wrong With the Intake Specialist, Receptionist and Call Center

1) Calls are too long call — time yourself to measure how long you're talking on each call. Focus on shortening each new call, otherwise you'll end up becoming friends and nothing more than a good conversationalist, not a sales guy, which equals zero sales. The www.IntakeAcademy.com coaches teach your team how to control the call, to redirect the conversation and how to compassionately interrupt the conversation to get it back on track.
2) Ask permission to speak when you call a prospect, no exceptions.
3) Dig deep; get inside the prospects' head. Identify the emotional pain. What prompted them to call? Listen for the personal motivator.
4) Practice PAUSING with each new call.
5) Interrupting and talking over prospects. Stop focusing on getting through your agenda for each call, which is a sign that you need to

reexamine your purpose. Your purpose should be to close as many appointments as possible. You can't find out what your prospects want and need if you interrupt them with your own thoughts.

6) You need to find out what it is about your offer that they don't like before you make multiple offers.

7) Listen to the prospects; what are they saying? Can you repeat back what they said in the exact words they used?

8) Pay close attention to the language and vocabulary of your prospect. This will help you to know what to do or say next and you'll certainly find out quickly how serious they are.

9) Practice slowing down your thoughts before you speak.

10) You're excited, which is understandable, but you're not allowing the prospect to finish sentences or thoughts at crucial discovery points of your conversation. Therefore, not only are you missing several buying signals, you're also not asking for the appointment.

11) Practice having a sense of urgency. Speed is critically important in all sales situations at every single point. If you have a sense of urgency in your voice, your prospect will.

12) Finally, you can do this, but first, you need to decide if you're in the game or not. But what you have to realize is that the telephone is the most time efficient, least expensive sales conversion, relationship building, communication and marketing tool you have.

Intake Specialist: Self-critiquing

At first your team, intake specialists, attorneys, investigators, case managers and call center will be resistant or timid that their phone calls are being recorded for training and quality assurance. If you're also going to do mystery calls (ghost calls), it's important that your team knows about that as well. As long as you're honest, positive and supportive of your team, it will become easier and easier for them to hear their own recorded phone calls and they will become experts at critiquing their own phone calls. Put a system in place that holds your team accountable for daily self-critiquing and scoring their recorded calls. As always, check the laws for recording phone calls in your state.

Best Practices of Telephone Etiquette

How to put someone on hold, how to transfer, language, call to action (CTA), how to take messages, repeat back, repeat phone numbers... you're the first responder. It's your job to make sure that your client and prospects get safely to the right person. Until you know that's happened, your job isn't done. Your script has been written and designed to guide you on how to handle all of this.

When putting someone on hold first... "Mary, I'm going to put you on hold for a moment while I go ahead and do xxx. Would that be okay?" Yes. Then, you can put them on hold. Then, quickly get right back to them... "Mary, thank you for holding, now you were saying xxx, right?" When you first get the call you still want a powerful love greeting, listen to what they say, tell them you can help them and then do the hold steps.

Put a system in place to monitor your call flow, everything that happens with your incoming calls (outbound prospective client sales calls and established client phone calls), how many you get per day, what type. Triage the calls, take care of each of them at that moment and put an ongoing inspection plan in place to always Inspect What You Expect™.

Callers Being Put on Hold

I understand you may have to put callers on hold, but it's critical that you know why, pay close attention, perhaps you can decrease the amount of hold time by discovering a problem on your team that can easily be fixed, for example, some team members maybe on "do not disturb" or several people at the same time have been scheduled to take a break, etc. What gets measured gets done, what you focus on expands, so, inspect what you expect, understand exactly why callers are being put on hold, why are callers hanging up, why are you having to take messages for callers to be called back later?

Trust transfer. How to transfer calls: "Mary, I'm going to transfer you to xxx and she'll/he'll take very good care of you, would that be okay?" Wait for reply and then go for it. To successfully complete the Intake Academy trust transfer, you must tell the person you're transferring the call to the name of the caller, the emotional state that person is in and what was the initial question she/he asked. Then it's the job of the next person to say, "Hello, Mary. Jane tells me you're calling today about xxx, right?" Yes. "I'm sorry to hear you've had an accident.

I hope you're okay. I'd like to welcome you to ABC Law," etc. Always check in on the person you put on hold if it's going to be longer than 15 seconds. Pay very close attention to the transferred call. Did Mary get connected okay? Did she hang up? It's your job as the first responder to make absolutely sure all calls get safely to the next step.

The first impressions director (first responder), receptionist, front desk is the advocate for all prospect and client phone calls and will do whatever is necessary to guarantee that each call safely arrives in the hands of the next team member. You fight for the client. Often, throughout your presentation with the prospect or client, repeat back what they say... "Mary, I'd like to interrupt you for a moment to be sure I understood what you just said, okay?" Yes. "Did you say... ?" It's critical that you listen and repeat back for a few reasons. It will help you to focus and stay on point with the caller, it will give you a mental rest, it will show the caller that you really do care, you get them, you listened and heard and it's important for them to hear back what they say they're calling for, what their problem is so they can be reminded how important it really is that they did call today. You should also do this with empathy and a sense of urgency, otherwise they may think it's not so important.

24 Secrets to Coach Your Team to Be Winners

1) WARNING: Stick to the phone script. Many times the receptionist or the intake specialist can get comfortable in their own routine. They start to feel confident, which is good, but for some it means they get lazy or complacent. This is normal human behavior. I compare it to myself and losing weight. I lost the weight I wanted because I finally accepted the fact I had to have a plan and be committed. I followed specific proven steps (script), then after several months of changing habits and behaviors, I got complacent thinking I've got this, I can do it. Before I really even knew it, I Slipped Back Into Old Bad Habits and Behaviors™. With the snap of a finger, I put 50 pounds back on. The intake specialist creates their own phone script instead of using the proven Intake Academy Relationship Conversion Script that they've been extremely successful with, which means they've lost focus on what works. Don't let this happen! The script that works is your best friend, influencing your prospective and established clients to do business with you — what they wanted to begin with or they wouldn't have called you.

If you get lazy about this and allow your team to deviate from the script, you run a big risk of losing many appointment opportunities and ultimately cases. Scripts work, so hold your feet to the fire.

> **Resource:** The single most important thing you can do to support your team and protect your marketing dollars is RMFD™ — Record, Monitor, Feedback, Daily — all your inbound phone calls. This will help hold your team accountable.

2) Provide a list of common objections with correct answers available.

3) Practice how to answer objections. Each time you prepare to launch a new campaign, put together a list of potential objections that your team might get and review that list with them. Prepare them to be excited about all the new calls they are going to receive.

4) Use a script, test your script and then keep using the one that works the best.

5) Practice how to use the script over and over again. Teach them how to sound, how to use their voice as a tool, their tone, their inflection — all without sounding scripted.

6) Make sure that your team knows everything about your business before they get on the phone.

> **Pop Quiz:** Ask your team, first impressions director, intake specialists, attorneys, senior level executives, case managers, call center, legal assistants — everyone from the front of the office to the back, from the top down — why the client should do business with your law firm.

7) Create testimonials that are appropriate for your practice that your team can quickly refer to. This helps to build their confidence, as well as sharing stories with prospective and established clients (of course without sharing confidential information). It's important to remind your team, often, of all the success that your firm is having by helping to change lives.

8) Coach your team on how to use testimonials; you can't just say, "Use this." Show them how they can weave different stories into their conversation.

9) Provide ongoing coaching, motivation and recognition. This is a must, because you're dealing with people. Coaching and mastermind groups works for you and your team needs coaching, too.

Chris Mullins and the Intake Academy of in-house certified coaches all become a member of your team.

10) Daily pop quizzes are a great way to keep your team focused, moving forward, motivated, sharp, excited and knowledgeable about your business.
11) Develop ongoing contests and bonuses. Keep score publicly for all team members to see.
12) Do the math. Track and talk about the sales numbers (appointments) daily with your team.
13) Teach your team how to focus on one call at time. Visualizing is a great tool for staying focused on the next call. Think about Mary, the next prospect in line to call. What does she look like, how can you be of service to Mary? How can YOU solve Mary's problem?
14) Voice message script. Create an outline for the messages your team will leave. Again, hold them accountable for using the script. Create scripts for everything that you do.
15) Provide headsets that work for your team. It's faster and easier for them to navigate and cuts down on fatigue.
16) Observe your team as they make calls. Listen carefully to the tone of voice. How are they doing, really? Watch their body language. Should they be in this position? Are they okay? Do they need a break?
17) Teach your team to use good listening techniques by paying attention to the tone, the voice, the breathing and background noise of the clients.
18) Case Management (CRM). Teach your team to use the system you have. Teach your team to keep detailed notes on each call, especially documenting the exact language and vocabulary of your prospects and clients.
19) Stop treating your receptionist, your intake specialist and case managers as low-level employees! Your inbound calls are critically important to your business. The inbound call gives the very first impression of your business. Pay attention to how your phone is being answered and monitor those calls to be sure you're capturing all sales opportunities. Give your team all the important ongoing coaching, training and information they need to be successful. Set them up to win, not fail. Imagine, for just a moment, that your entire team didn't come to work today. Now what?

20) First, you must decide that the first impressions director, the receptionist, the intake team is critically important to your business. Roll out the red carpet! Stop dealing with turnover. Sell with integrity from the top down. The way you treat your internal team (internal customers) is exactly how your team will treat your external customers.

21) Monitor all team members that use the phone. There's no way around this, you must Inspect What You Expect™. However, you must go at this from a positive point of view. The purpose of monitoring calls is to listen to them to identify all the great things that are happening so you can repeat them and all the areas that need to be tweaked fast. It depends on how you view this strategy and then how you break the news to your staff about this new way of coaching. In fact, this technique is the fastest way you can grow your business and keep it growing.

22) Teach self-critiquing. Your entire team must know how to critique their own phone calls and provide you with feedback.

23) Implement a bonus plan (commission works best) that promotes MORE business which will make even more money for your receptionist, intake specialists, call center and all team members that touch the phone.

24) Have fun! Don't give up. You can do this!

Put Your Entire Team Through Role-playing Based on PAS (Problem, Agitate, Solution)

A top salesperson not only knows WHAT sales is — how to use and apply PAS, close, follow up, build relationships, time management, multi-task, knows and understands the power of words — he or she must also have the voice (tone) and know how to use it during all points of communication with each and every prospect and member.

How to Become a Master Closer With PAS

The PAS formula has been around forever and used by all top sales business owners. I'm sure many of you have seen this before, but the question is, do you actually use it in your business? Here's a great trial close example:

If I show you how you _____, would you be interested in knowing more?

Before you can trial close, you've got to know why they're calling you today. Get inside their head. Ask questions and *listen*.

Try the PAS Formula

Many of you have probably already heard of PAS. With this formula, you first state a problem and secure the prospect's agreement that the problem exists.

Next, you get the prospect agitated about the problem. [PAUSE]

Finally, you produce the solution. "Wouldn't it be wonderful if there was an alternative to protect you from those daily surprises?" [PAUSE]. Try this team exercise.

Team Exercise: Try this team exercise in your next weekly sales drill.

The problem: _____

Agitation: _____

Solution: _____

The problem: _____

Agitation: _____

Solution: _____

The problem: _____

Agitation: _____

Solution: _____

The problem: _____

Agitation: _____

Solution: _____

Chapter 3: *Chris Mullins*

Know Your Numbers!
Mullins' Tour de France (not!)

I'm getting a baseline for my cycling. Wow! I'm so excited, I've been searching and searching and have finally found a personal trainer for cycling. His name is Dan and he and I meet twice a week.

Our first meeting was basic fitness information, measuring my bike, checking my bike out, asking health questions and taking my measurements. Next, we'll be doing a three- and five-minute time trial to get a baseline of my current performance — sound familiar?

My long-term goal is to complete a 100-mile race. That's a 12-week training program and I can't wait! My short term goals are different each week.

More on Chris' Personal Cycling Trainer and How It Relates to Your Law Firm

This guy is really big on the numbers. The numbers tell all; they quantify everything that I do on my bicycle.

The first day, I had a three-mile time trial (a 5K) on my indoor trainer. I know I already mentioned this to you, but I felt like Lance Armstrong; you know that face, that serious, focused, disciplined look.

I'm not sure why, but when I'm on my indoor trainer, I am much more focused when I look down at the floor. Maybe it's because that's when I'm in that pushing zone, the sweet spot. It isn't easy, but I really love pushing myself.

Dan had his stopwatch and was asking me where my level of exertion performance was at — hard, very hard or extremely difficult. The idea for three miles was to go as fast as I could while pacing myself to finish.

As I mentioned earlier, Dan is trying to get a baseline for my current performance level so he knows what my weekly goals need to be to get to my final ultimate goal — the big race.

Next, he'll create a customized training schedule that's made up of cycling, and because I enjoy running, he'll include that along with the three-mile runs I already have scheduled.

Dan can now create weekly goals for me with a new higher goal each week all to get me to that century ride in the best possible shape. Each week we'll ride together and monitor my progress. In one month we'll do another three-mile time trial to see how I have improved.

Know your numbers. Know what gets you excited and motivated to push each day to be a top-performing person, not just in sales and business, but in life. It's up to you — not your family, your friends or your boss. I was asked by a client, "How do I motivate my team?" My response is you really can't, they have to be self-motivated. Of course, you need a system in place for hiring correctly, but setting that aside, there are some things that you can do to initiate and foster a healthy, motivating, reward-team, focused environment. For starters, get to know your team individually (all of them). Ask what motivates them. Ask them to really give it some thought and get back to you.

Hint: It's not money. Tell them they can't come back to you with the old standby; a raise or money. To help them figure it out, share what really motivates you. As always, have a list of questions, thoughts and ideas in front of you. This means you need to *prepare* before you schedule time to talk to them.

Get in the habit of catching people doing things right. You, the attorney, managing partner, CEO, COO, may personally feel like, "For crying out loud, we're all adults. Why do I have to tell them they did a good job? Why do I have to keep training them? Shouldn't they know all of this by now?" No. One thing you have to understand as the business owner — the leader, the manager — is that you're dealing with people; we're all human, we make mistakes, we have another life besides work. We have baggage, bad habits and self-defeating behaviors. As long as you decide to continue working with people, you need to become more educated on how to coach and work with them. You're in the lifelong learning and teaching business.

> **Resource: Take the Intake Academy First Impressions Directors' Oath.** I, Chris Mullins, the first impressions director (first responder), receptionist, front desk team member will go to any length to absolutely make sure all client and prospective client phone calls are taken care of correctly. I understand that the real purpose of my job is to be the advocate for every single phone call and to protect each call. I have been empowered to do whatever is necessary to guarantee that each call safely arrives in the hands of the next team member. I will uphold this oath to whatever length is necessary. To learn more call (603) 924-1640 or visit www.IntakeAcademy.com.

Scripts and How to Use Them

Here's an example of several students showing their scripts. Notice how they even have one in the bathroom!

Chapter 3: *Chris Mullins*

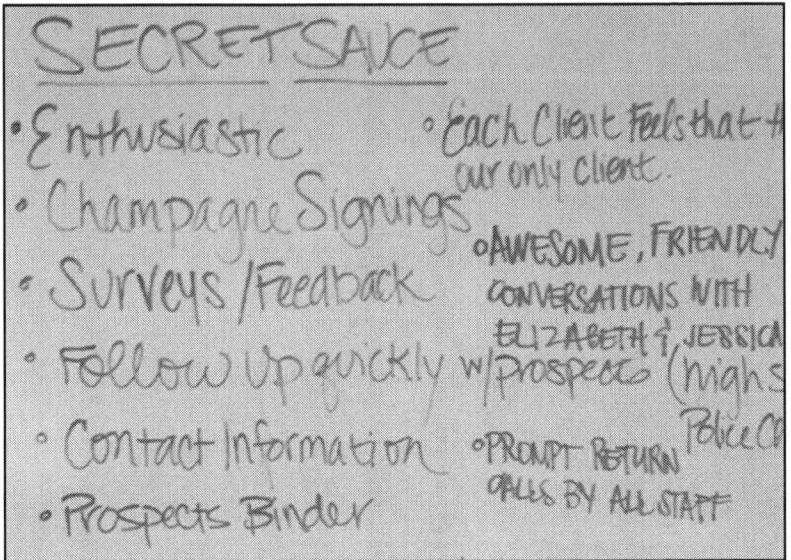

These four pictures demonstrate how the team at Geiger Law Office has their scripts placed near the phone and on their desks. The photo below is the secret sauce list written on the white board about why they feel they've been so successful.

SECRET SAUCE

- Enthusiastic
- Champagne Signings
- Surveys/Feedback
- Follow up quickly
- Contact Information
- Prospects Binder

○ Each Client Feels that our only client.
○ AWESOME, FRIENDLY CONVERSATIONS WITH ELIZABETH & JESSICA w/Prospect (nighs Police C
○ PROMPT RETURN CALLS BY ALL STAFF

Chapter 3: *Chris Mullins* 127

Your Most Important Tool

The single most important tool you can use in your business, in all parts of your business, not just the phone (hint, hint), you could script out your day to eliminate time vampires, but we're talking about the phone here. Folks that aren't hired to be hardcore sales closers hate scripts, they hate the "S" word and the other "S" word — sales — because they don't want to be phony, lie or sound like a robot with no feelings or empathy.

When you're in the Intake Academy Relationship, Sales, Conversion Phone Coaching Program (www.IntakeAcademy.com), you're taught how to do this. You don't have to read the script word for word, but there are some very important words, sentences on your script, certain language for a reason. A script is just a guide, a cheat sheet, a road map to guide you accurately to the next step while staying focused on what the sole purpose is, to close the deal. We're only human so it's easy to get sidetracked, off track, to steer the call into an entirely different direction other than closing the deal.

Here's exactly what we teach our students to do when it's time to learn a new script. In fact, I do this myself. I use scripts all the time but I don't sound scripted. 1) Get a recorder and read your script into your recorder three different times. Pick the best one, then delete the others. 2) Listen to the recording every single day a minimum of three times per day for 10 consecutive days. That's while you fall asleep, while you're on the treadmill, while you're driving in your car. We recently had a 10-Day Voice Lesson Script Challenge for our members. It was an incredible opportunity for those that stepped up to the plate. 3) After 10 days, test yourself. If your calls are recorded, listen to them. Did you LEAP ahead? If you don't have recordings, have one of your teammates do a difficult role-play with you. No excuses — find a way to test yourself. Did you LEAP ahead? Also, record the role-play and listen to it over and over again. Real sales athletes never stop role-playing or listening to their recordings or practicing new scripts. They do it daily to stay sharp, more often when they're trying to learn a new one quickly.

Mindset

I'd like to start this chapter by saying that without the intake specialist, you have no business. I think we can all agree that you're in business because you want to do good. However, this is a business and the mindset of the owner/attorney is critical with regards to the bottom line, but even more critical is the "sales mindset" of the receptionist and intake specialist. You can love what you do, still be a sales expert and still want to improve the bottom line of the business.

Maybe a Chris Mullins True Personal Story From the Good Old Days Will Help

My first real job (30-plus years ago) was working as an inside salesperson for the classified advertising department of a large newspaper.

This job was a very big deal to me because it was the major newspaper in the town I grew up in. Whenever I drove by the *Lawrence Eagle Tribune* in N. Andover, Mass., it seemed so big to me. Wouldn't it be great to work there someday?

I got the job and was there for several months and I thought I was incredible, the best — I really felt very strongly that I finally understood many of the important points of the job.

The big winner for me was how I handled the customers. I was unstoppable! No one could match the service I gave to each and every customer that called the classified advertising department. I felt very good about what I did each day. I have arrived.

Chris' Big Thought

Business owners, attorneys pay close attention to the above message. In many cases this is how your team feels because you haven't taught them any different. Phil, my boss, didn't teach me either, or at least as often as he should have. Therefore, I thought my job was to do everything possible to make the customer happy, which to me meant save the customer money and keep them laughing and talking.

How do you measure up? Are you creating automatic production machines with the right language, Sales Talk™ and ongoing coaching in your business? Or, are you sending the wrong message just like Phil did? You've got to continually remind, police, support and coach your entire team.

The Rest of My Story...

Phil called me into his office and basically told me what a bad job I was doing. I was embarrassed and became very angry because I honestly had no idea. Phil's concern was that I was on the phone too long with customers, talking up a storm, not controlling the conversation and saving them money on their classified ads.

After that talk I really disliked the newspaper and wasn't happy at my job anymore because I really believed that the paper was out to steal from the customer.

As time passed and I attended various newspaper association sales conferences, I quickly learned that Phil was right. I was actually doing a disservice by trying to save advertisers money, because I wasn't giving them the opportunity to write the best story ever about what they wanted to sell, which meant it would get better, more qualified readership and they would have more opportunity to sell.

I realized that the longer I was on the phone with one customer the more I was hurting others waiting to be taken care of that were on hold or had simply hung up. I learned the hard way, but I did learn and that was the beginning of my true understanding of sales, the sales presentation and selling with integrity. I learned that customer service *is* sales. Sales *is* customer service. Selling to the customer's specific need and emotional pain the problem to solve *is* customer service.

Self-Motivation & Self-Discipline: The Discovery Mindset

As I've mentioned in the past, the common denominator that I've found and read about for folks that remain at the top — whether professionally or personally, whether top senior executives or frontline staff members — are those that continually educate, challenge and push themselves, the receptionist and the entire team to learn something new every day.

In addition, the team that remains at the top isn't just dedicated to learning something new, but they're committed and they're self-disciplined enough to apply what they've learned and go from there. They take action!

I'm not talking about the people who always score the highest on tests or college exams, I'm talking about everybody and anybody; you don't need a high IQ to develop your own personal system for being self-motivated and self-disciplined.

Some of you may say, "Every day?" Yes! Every day. You can learn so much about yourself AND those around you, every day.

There are lessons in everything we do and say, all that we hear and see others do. However, unless you, the business owner/attorney, are in the mindset of continually learning, asking yourself the question, "How can I apply what I just heard or read to my own situation?" you will not be in the mindset of discovery and neither will your team.

One of the easiest and quickest ways to get your team into this discovery mindset (which is, of course, a new habit that you'll need to develop) is to simply encourage them to ask questions.

Ask questions of those around you. Many times we hear things that others say that we don't get, we don't understand, but we just push it aside; sometimes we even try to look like we get it.

Usually this happens because we're either intimidated ("They'll think I'm stupid") or we may be thinking, "I don't see the value in understanding what I just heard, it doesn't apply to me." Here are just a few ideas on how you can begin to get yourself and your team into the mindset of discovery.

1) Read. Read for fun. Read to understand more about your profession. Read to understand more about your client's emotional buying behaviors. Read to learn about everything else.

2) Ask questions. Get into the habit of asking more questions of those around you, but don't forget you must also LISTEN to the answers.

3) Start a book club for all team members in the firm to attend — a firm-wide book club with help your team grow, to work on their sales mindset, the business bottom line, their clients and customer service. This is a great way to get comfortable with others. Put yourself and your team in a situation where you will read, discuss books, learn about yourself and other people at the same time.

4) Join Toastmasters. Get involved with an organized professional group or club that will stimulate you to step out of your comfort zone, learn and grow. This is an excellent resource I recommend for developing great speaking skills and presentation skills, both of which help the bottom line. (Go to www.toastmasters.org.)

5) Get a journal. Journal writing for professional and personal discoveries is like an ongoing, do-it-yourself, self-development training course. Write down your thoughts, feelings, discoveries, lessons and daily successes. Members of our "Get MullinSIZED Phone Success Training Program have either Sales Success Journals™ (SSJ) or Personal Success Journals™ (PSJ) — some have both. Find out more about these at www.GreatBottomLine.com.

6) Review your journal often — daily, weekly and monthly.

7) Goals. Set goals for yourself, put together a step-by-step action plan, add a start date, a deadline and be prepared to tweak along the way. Don't give up. Just do it!

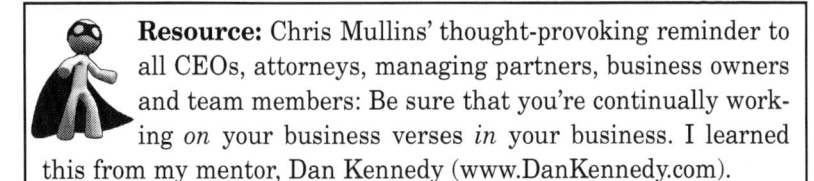

> **Resource:** Chris Mullins' thought-provoking reminder to all CEOs, attorneys, managing partners, business owners and team members: Be sure that you're continually working *on* your business verses *in* your business. I learned this from my mentor, Dan Kennedy (www.DanKennedy.com).

Customer Service IS Sales

As the business owner, the leader, you have to get this. Then you need to quickly make sure that your receptionist and the entire team gets it. They simply have to be comfortable with the "S" word. In fact, you should all sing the word SALES over and over again at the top of your lungs, daily.

Understanding how true this really is that customer service is sales is the absolute quickest, easiest way to influence your team into becoming strong salespeople with integrity. Many clients share with me that they can't get Mary to sell because she says, "I'm not a salesperson. You didn't hire me to be a salesperson. I'm the receptionist, I just answer the phone."

Customer service taught correctly will get you the best of both worlds, but you do have to say the S word — S A L E S. Did you know...

1) Clients hear 50% of what you say and 100% of how you feel.

2) Clients are usually intimidated and they'll "yes" you when they don't really understand what you're saying to them.

3) Assume nothing.

4) Understand the importance of returning messages, email, telephone and fax. Do what you say you'll do!

5) Learn how to listen to your clients.

Make the decision for the client — that's what they want. Remember that your goal is to be of service to your clients and prospects. People need to be told what to do for a variety of reasons, but at the top would be the lack of confidence in their own decision-making ability. They may lack self-esteem, self-confidence and have a history of making the wrong decision. Assume the sale. That's what your prospects and clients want. They trust you and want you to tell them what to do.

The "S" Word (Sales)

Make life easy for yourself — save time and energy — and start from the beginning.

Hire people who can sell or will be okay with selling, meaning, not offended by it. It's more important to hire people who understand sales, the bottom line, sales targets, scripts, goals and business than it is to hire those experienced in your business.

It's time to yell and scream at the top of your lungs the "S" word. Say it right now!

SALES
SALES
SALES

Put up "What did you sell today?" signs (everybody should have those everywhere, except, of course, where your clients will see them).

In fact, you (the owner/attorney) and each team member must talk sales (Sales Talk™) everyday, no exceptions!

I'll begin by saying I LOVE SALES and I believe in sales and teach sales. I help folks like you identify sales moments. Think about it for a moment. We're all born salespeople, naturally trying to convince others of what we believe to be true and of what we want, trying to change beliefs, and in many cases we don't even realize it. Everything we do in our life involves sales. In fact, sales should be taught early on in junior high school, it would make life so much easier for students and it would make them better applicants in the job world which would help us all.

Sales is training for life, from trying to convince your partner of some new high-priced gizmo you want to buy, to convincing your daughter's teacher that even though she may have Attention Deficit Disorder you fully expect the team of teachers to work just as hard for her future success as they do with all other students, to convincing the store manager of a retail store that you expect a complete refund, etc.

There are good and bad apples out there; bad salespeople who lie, who don't care about anything they sell or the people they sell to. Then there's you and me; we love what we do and believe in it, but at the end of the day we know we must sell, increase our herd of prospective clients and retain our established clients or we're out of business. Basically, as long as you do your homework and match the right products and services to your interested prospects and established clients, you're golden. That's sales and, of course, you never give up. In fact, if you don't continually offer your prospects and established clients more products and services, whether they ask for them or not, you're doing them a disservice. They deserve to know what you have available and they deserve the opportunity to believe that they're worthy of them, so give them a chance!

It's important to help your entire staff — not just the receptionist, the intake specialist, the case managers — understand what sales is really about. It's about customer service, it's upselling and it's sharing all your services and products with your prospects and clients.

Where Does the Receptionist and Intake Specialist Come In?

Your phone rings and the caller says, "Are you taking new clients?" It doesn't matter why they call. If they called, they want to do business with you, now, and you must grab them by the shirt collar and pull them through the phone. Guide them and tell them what decision to make (which is, for example, to make an appointment). An easy way to do this is to say...

"Terrific! Mrs. Smith, you made the right decision calling ABC Law today. My name is Chris and it's nice to meet you. I have an opportunity for you to meet personally with the attorney today at 10:00 am."

Your job, purpose, goal and focus with each and every call is to ask for the sale. For some of you that's appointments in person, for others it's appointments by phone. It may mean investigators going to the home of the prospective client others or even mailing a new client wel-

> **Resource:** All communication moments with clients are Sales Moments™. To learn more about our comprehensive sales conversion coaching, call (603) 924-1640 or email beth@intakeacademy.com.

come kit with instructions on what the next step is. The bottom line is, know what the desired outcome is for all prospect calls, then just do it. In many cases you'll ask three times in one conversation. This is how you make the decision for the client.

Challenge Your Team

Many salespeople currently sell due to habit. If they're used to selling 20 appointments a day and no one is challenging them, that's exactly what they'll sell. It's all about habits and behaviors! Your confidence and comfort zone, of course, are part of the equation as well.

"You're NOT Your Client" Staff Exercise

The purpose of the exercise below (which I received from a colleague) is to help the receptionist and all team members better understand their clients by putting themselves in the client's shoes. To be reminded of what it's like to be a client. To keep top of mind, on a daily basis, your "purpose." Many times I've recommended this type of exercise to clients, students and members of our Intake Academy phone sales coaching program (See the Team Exercise on the next page.)

I once did a teleseminar for one of our private clients on attitude, smiling and mindset. I thought I'd share a few of the highlights.

1) View yourself as a Sales Business Owner (SBO) — the expert of the telephone.

2) Understand that your purpose is sales. At the end of the day that's all that really matters. What did you sell today? How many appointments did you sell?

3) Know specifically what works for you and do more of it. Know your strengths. Craft your presentation, your script, your message to each prospective and established client, tweak where necessary until you have the secret presentation that you know works. Bulldoze through life's challenges!

4) Sharpen your axe, whether you're a seasoned professional or a new recruit. Compete with yourself by asking, "How can I tweak that just a little more to save more time, sell more, cross-sell, upsell, shorten the sales cycle, get more referrals or manage my customer accounts and time more efficiently?"

5) Examine and develop ways for you — the sales professional (and celebrity customer sales coordinator) — to stand out amongst all the rest at your business, in your industry and more importantly from every other business out there that your clients and prospective clients communicate with day in and day out. Smile, make the call and sell something™!

When Things Go Wrong

When things go wrong, as they sometimes will,
When the road you're trudging seems all up hill,
When the finds are low and the debts are high,
And you want to smile, but you have to sigh,
When care is pressing you down a bit,
Rest, if you must, but don't you quit.
Life is queer with its twists and turns,
As every one of us sometimes learns,
And many a failure turns about
When he might have won had he stuck it out;
So don't give up, though the pace seems slow –
For you may succeed with another blow.
Often the goal is nearer than
It seems to a faint and faltering man,
Often the struggler has given up,
When he might have captured the victor's cup.
And he learned too late, when the night slipped down,
How close he was to the golden crown.
Success is failure, turned inside out –
The silver tint of the clouds of doubt –
And you never can tell how close you are,
It may be near when it seems afar;
So stick to the fight when you're hardest hit –
It's when things seem worst that you mustn't quit!

– author unknown

> **Team Exercise:** For one week team members should take the list below and keep track of their own personal experiences with customer service at the places they frequent over seven days — food shopping, online shopping, restaurants, movies, clothes shopping, banks, call centers, using the telephone to get personal projects and errands done, etc. Next, associates should share with the group how they would translate the experiences they had to the job they do every day.
>
> 1) How did you feel?
>
> 2) Did you feel welcome?
>
> 3) Did you feel rushed?
>
> 4) Were you made to feel as if you were the only person in the store?
>
> 5) Was your sales associate helpful?
>
> 6) If not, did they find someone who could help you easily?
>
> 7) Did your sales/customer service associate know their product?
>
> 8) Did you yourself discover the answers to your questions?
>
> 9) Did they introduce themselves and approach you well?
>
> 10) Did they help you buy, or did they let you buy?
>
> 11) Did you feel positive control from the intake specialist?
>
> 12) Did they add on sales?
>
> 13) Was their help useful?
>
> 14) Was it what you expected, less than or more than?
>
> *Email your results to beth@intakeacademy.com to get feedback from Chris.*

Three Words to Keep Top of Mind

Webster's Dictionary defines...

RELAX – *to unwind, loosen up, to rest*

The sales, customer service or business environment isn't for relaxing. The idea is to have a sales team full of energy, love what they do, but know and believe at the end of the day it's about sales and scheduling appointments. The receptionist, along with the rest of the team, is excited and full of ideas; a team that believes in themselves as individuals and as a team. If you relax while playing the sales game, you'll take your eye off the ball, you'll slip up, miss a beat and you won't have both eyes on your focus and your purpose. At the end of the day all that really matters is... What did you sell?

COMPLACENT – *satisfied, self-satisfied, smug, unworried, content, self-righteous*

Be very careful, our students hear me speak of this often. Complacency is a life struggle for many professionals; a struggle to be able to quickly identify when complacency decides to show its ugly head. Don't be fooled; it shows up when you least expect it.

If you don't allow yourself to relax while playing the sales game, you won't be able to combat complacency. You'll always be focused and remain sharp.

READINESS – *willingness, gameness, eagerness, promptness, speediness*

Be ready the moment you drive into your office parking lot. Teach and guide your team to be ready for business daily.

The idea is to shake off everything that happened before you got into the office. It's game time! A great way to get ready is to have a "sales huddle" first thing every morning, five days a week, without fail. The attorney/owner/manager and all team members should do this to get ready for the day and have each team member share very quickly and concisely, in 10 minutes or less...

1) What they sold yesterday.

2) What they plan on selling today.

3) What they're forecasting for sales (appointments, packets mailed, outbound sales phone calls, successfully singing and checking in during the intake screening process) for the week.

4) How they'll do it — specifically.

Keep the tone businesslike, positive and motivational. It's a sales huddle and everyone stands. They're charged up with a clear focus on the (daily) goal; their purpose — sales targets!

> **Resource:** To join Chris Mullins' Monday Morning Sales Huddle, email beth@intakeacademy.com or call (603) 924-1640.

So, You Think You're a Salesperson?

Here's what doesn't make a good salesperson. Instead, you've become an excellent conversationalist. Just because you like the business you work for, you have a pleasant-sounding voice and you're courteous to the prospective client, it doesn't make you a salesperson.

What's most important and missing from the above is, are you a CLOSER? Do you understand that your job is to sell appointments? Can you close? Or do you just take no for an answer and say, "Call us when you're ready?"

You've got to get past all the client service-type attitude stuff like, "I'll be nice and they will come or they'll call us when they're ready." This isn't the case; your clients and prospective clients want to be sold, that's why they called you. They want you to tell them what to do. They want you to take them by the hand and make the decision easy for them.

Again, at the end of the day all that really matters is how many more appointments did you sell today than yesterday?

Now that you realize you need help in sales, ask for it. Get sales coaching from the attorney, other top-performing individuals in your office or even the manager. Remember, the manager has to understand sales and how to sell. This is advanced selling that we teach at www.IntakeAcademy.com.

An excellent way to coach the intake specialist, the receptionist, the attorney, owner and other team members on how to focus on closing sales is to record calls and presentations, then listen to and critique them. This is the most important step and piece of information that I use in all of my training with owners and staff. You can do this, too.

Remember to always Inspect What You Expect™ in all aspects of your business. It's especially important with all the thousands (even millions) of dollars you're spending on marketing just to get your phones to ring and to get prospects to opt-in to your web sites.

Great! The phones are ringing! Leads are funneling through the sys-

> **Resource:** Call Monitoring Inspection Program. For those of you who do not want sales training services, but do want your phone calls monitored and results reported to senior level executives, email beth@intakeacademy.com and put HERO MONITORING in the subject line or call (603) 924-1640.

tem. Now what? The Intake Academy team Inspects What You Expect with your team or call center, including fixing the problem areas your team and/or call center is having have been solved by others.

Close the Deal in Two Ways

There are two sales opportunities on every single call. And in some scripts there are three — you ask for referrals. However, with relationship building closing scripts, you can't just add whatever you want when you feel like it. With some scripts you have to make sure that it won't upset the flow or the real desired outcome of the phone call.

There are two sales opportunities in every prospect phone call. One, close the sale. Whatever the sale is in your firm, do it. Remember, that's why they called. They need your help and to them, at this very moment, you are their lifeline.

If for some reason, that cannot be accomplished, move quickly with the same assumptive tone, sense of urgency and mindset to sales opportunity two, which is explained on the Intake Academy, Relationship, Sales and Conversion Script.

Here's an example of sales opportunity two: "Mary, since you're not ready to make the appointment today, I'm going to send you our **FREE** book, *The 7 Secrets to Choosing Law Firms That Win Because They Care*. What's your mailing address?

Hanging up with at least the contact information is critical so that first and foremost the firm can keep this lead, that has cost $200.00 to $500.00 marketing dollars just to get this ONE prospect to call, in your marketing funnel to receive your marketing. material. Get the appointment or whatever you consider your sale to be with the prospect call. Get the complete contact information, the mailing address, two phone numbers, email and possibly a referral. If you hang up with NO appointment and NO contact information then this was not a successful call. Financially you're hemorrhaging because of the $500-plus cost just to get the phone to ring and then you hang up with zero.

Resource: For more information on the Intake Sales Specialist Hiring System, go to www.IntakeAcademy.com or email beth@intakeacademy.com for more information.

The Truth About Intake Specialists — The Real Heroes of the Law Firm

"We have met the enemy... and he is us." — Pogo

Hero – *a person, who is admired or idealized for courage, outstanding achievements or noble qualities.*

The doctor called me and said you have to make a decision right this minute. Either your husband dies or we amputate both of his legs. What do you want us to do?

My sister is the hospital right now dying at any moment now from cancer I don't know what to do. Help me, what should I do?

Attorneys, stop what you're doing at this moment, drop everything and take just a moment to imagine that you just found out your entire team of intake specialists, regardless of the size of your firm, didn't show up for work today. What would you do? Really, what would your first thought be? What would your first action step be?

Do you take your team for granted? The truth is that your team doesn't really think you care anymore, they don't think you understand what they go through all day long. The intake team is the glue that keeps your firm together. Without your intake team (receptionist, master of first impressions, front desk) you have no law firm, you're out of business.

Here are just some of the feelings your intake specialists (they share these feelings during our intake coaching sessions), your team, has about your prospects and clients: complacency, entitlement, judgment, they're not deserving, they're lying, faking, they're pitiful, they're crazy, they're drunk, they're mental cases.

The prospect told me he/she wanted to shoot him/herself. I tried to calm them down, I was scared out of my mind. I didn't know what to

> **Resource:** Hire individuals to work in your business that focus on sales — that's it. Someone to protect the sales process, all the steps involved and will be the point of contact (they must be well versed in presentation skills). To learn more about the Intake Academy hiring, screening and selection process, email beth@intakeacademy.com or call (603) 924-1640.

do. I've been taught to listen, be compassionate, to let them know I'm glad they called me today, you made the right decision calling, you're not alone. Then, three days later, I find out he did kill himself.

Attorneys, how does your team live with that? Do you listen to the phone calls your team is taking all day long? You should, because it will keep you focused on what life is like for the prospect, the client, and what a day in the life of an intake specialist is really like.

Intake specialists, every day, all day long, phone call after phone call — whether personal injury, SSD, mass tort, criminal, divorce, all practice niche areas — your team listens to the stories and pain from others. But now that your team has been doing it for so long they may think of the prospect and client as the mentals or the mental cases, for example.

Attorneys, I'm worried about your team. This is something I think of all the time and say out loud to my clients. Recently, after listening to a prospective attorney that wanted to be our client, I said to her, "I hear everything you're saying about why you can't get your team to do what you want. Or, that your phones just have to go to voice mail if they're ringing off the hook, or hey I'll just fire them all and start over. I understand the challenges you face with your business and your team. I understand how it's easier to look the other way, but when we do this we're hemorrhaging because you're spending thousands, and many of you millions of dollars, on marketing to get your phones to ring, to get prospects to opt-in, but you're spending *no time, money or effort* at all on inspecting what happens when it does. What happens to all those leads you paid for? What's being said on the intake call? What's being said by the attorney? Are the outbound calls being made? What happens with the lead comes in via the internet? That's what we call hemorrhaging."

Then I looked at the client and said, "Out of everything you're sharing with me, the only thing I'm really worried about is your team. I'm very concerned for them."

Here's why. Below are a list of questions that we always ask the team during our Intake Academy coaching.

- How many of you have been the client? *Many raise their hand.*
- How many of you have family or friends that have been the client? *Several raise their hand.*
- How many of you could have been the client? *Some raise their hand.*
- How many of you have medical degrees? *No one raises their hand.*

- How many of you are psychologists? *No one raises their hand.*
- How many of you have degrees in crisis management? *No one raises their hand.*
- How many of you have worked on a suicide hotline? *No one raises their hand..*

Wow! Sit with those results for just a moment. Imagine that! Yet every single one of your intake team members (receptionist, front desk, etc.) are on the phone all day long sitting in a small cubicle in a chair, taking call after call listening to screaming, yelling, swearing, suicide threats, abuse, crying, my husband just walked out the door with my kids, I have no food to put on the table tonight. Why won't you help me? Why won't the case manager call me back? What am I going to do? My father ran over my daughter with the car by accident. My brother is dying, 95% of his body is burned, he has a 3-year-old daughter, what should I do? I'm sleeping next to the dumpster with my kids again tonight.

Here's just a small example of what Chris Mullins and our team of experienced in-house certified Intake Academy coaches work on with your team. We coach the intake specialist (receptionist, front desk and call center) to take responsibility for their own habits and behaviors. For example: If you're stressed or having a meltdown, regardless of the reason (perhaps a combination of work and home), you must find a way to reframe it. To remind yourself that you're a gift. You're the lifeline, the rock for that person you're speaking to. When they call you it's because they need a lifeline. They're on the edge, and that edge is different for everyone, but it's their edge they're living with and suffering through.

The career you're in is to be of service. You're not in the legal business as much as you're in the relationship and healing business. You've gotten to be so conditioned and into an automatic routine that you don't even think about the person on the phone, rather "I need to

> **Resource:** Limited time slots available on a first come, first served basis for your **FREE** Attorney Conversion Consult with Chris Mullins. This appointment is for the attorney. Chris will play the mystery call for the attorney and share exactly what you need to do to fix any problem areas. To schedule your confidential mystery call consult, email beth@intakeacademy.com or call (603) 924-1640.

hurry to get to the next one." Then you have the attorneys, the partners that have metrics they want you to meet each month. Of course, this is a business and without sales you have no business, therefore you have no job.

Attorneys, support your team, be of service to your team and give them all the coaching you possibly can so they can do the same for your prospects and client — one relationship, one phone call at a time. Provide Intake Academy venting lounges (quiet rooms) for your team to have a safe place to go to calm down, to rest, to be quiet, to vent feelings with no repercussions so that they can get ready for the next call.

Resource: To get more information on International Intake Specialist Week™, the Legal Intake Specialist Association™ (LISA) Boot Camp and Legal Intake Specialist 911™, call (603) 924-1640 or email beth@intakeacademy.com. Refer to page 176 in this book.

AHA Notes:

Chapter *Four*

FAQs With Chris Mullins

Beth Wolfson Asks Chris Some FAQs

Wolfson: Hey, Chris, one of the questions we get from our clients is why isn't my team using the script I gave them?

Mullins: Because you haven't coached them on how to use it, you haven't taught them how to use it. They have no idea what you want from them.

Wolfson: So what you're saying is the attorney can't just give them the script? We came up with these screening questions and they're on three sheets of paper and we have three different areas that we're focusing on, and I gave it to them. I also gave them a greeting to say, but they don't always say the greeting and they don't always ask all the screening questions. Why won't they do it?

Mullins: As long as the attorney decides to stay in business with human beings, you can't just give them a piece of paper and say, "Do it." They're not machines, so what you need to do is coach them. You need to give them the piece of paper and say, "Here's what it's for, here's why I want you to do it, here's each question, what the purpose is for each question and here's the desired outcome we're looking for.

> As long as the attorney decides to stay in business with human beings, you can't just give them a piece of paper and say, "Do it."

"Now let me teach you and show you how to use the question, how to say it, how to sound, when to pause, how to bob and weave and navigate the call and jump around on lily pads because the client or the prospect is taking you down another path." You can't just do that. You have to coach and train them and teach them over a period of time. What are your thoughts about that?

Wolfson: Because people are afraid of scripts. People don't like the word script. If you give somebody a script, with the exception of some people, here's what I think will happen. You have two camps of people where this is how it will shake out over a period of time. You'll have one camp of people who will follow the script to a T, robotically, they will sound like a call center, but they will try to comply absolutely as best they possibly can and they may sound that way. So if they are using the script, they may not sound like they're using it in a very good way. You'll have some people who fall into that category.

You have some people who genuinely want to comply. They will start to use the script that you give to them and then they will stop at some point or another because the prospect or the caller is taking them in another direction and they don't know how to divert the caller back to stay on script, so they let it go.

No one is paying attention to the fact that they're not following the script over a period of time. What happens is the script becomes this archaic piece of paper that collects dust, but it's part of the policy manual or it's part of yet another initiative that you started at your law firm that was given. One week it was, "All right, we're really excited about doing this."

And then two months down the road, three months down the road, whenever it is, it has become something that's just fallen by the wayside. Ultimately there may be some core elements from the original script that are still being used, and as you walk around the law firm, you may occasionally hear those things. So you are telling yourself in the back of your mind, "Yeah, the script is being used."

But until you chime in and listen to what's happening, most likely the script is not being used. But the reason why it doesn't get used is because people don't feel comfortable using scripts all the time, particularly if they're not held accountable to use it.

They don't feel comfortable using it from the outset and they're not taught how to use it the right way to keep callers essentially on script or in line when they get off script.

A lot of people just don't feel comfortable with that. They feel you're, in a way, infringing on their ability to communicate because communicating one-on-one in a conversation is a very personal thing, it's a very natural thing. It's very hard to tell someone, "Here's the way I want you to talk." When you do that with people, it makes them feel uncomfortable, so there has to be a lot more support as to why you're saying what you're saying. You have to give them a structure and a path. And then you have to help them to be successful and use whatever it is that you gave them.

Mullins: Right, and the other thing I'll add is the big picture is, which is quite simple follow, is the attorney didn't a hire a salesperson when they hired Mary or John to be a receptionist, front desk, or intake. You didn't put in your advertisement that you wanted a salesperson or who had that kind of experience or background.

So now when you say that you're going to use a script, they're thinking you're saying, "I'm now a salesperson." They're going to resist it because that's not what they took the job for.

Wolfson: Chris, how do you convince someone to be a client? Aren't they simply qualified or not?

Mullins: First off, if the team uses the intake screening questions and the relationship conversion script properly, you shouldn't have to convince someone. They're calling you because they need help and they're ready. And if you use your intake screening questions, you're going to know if they're qualified or not to get to the next step.

If you also have your relationship conversion script, your sales script, which is what we use at the Intake Academy, you're building a relationship with them, you're bonding with them emotionally. You have a level of intimacy, you're finding out the real reason they called today, like if they had a car accident. So if somebody does qualify and they start to back off, you could say, "Wait a minute, please don't do that. You made the right decision when you gave us a call. We are the right law firm for you. I know this seems really scary, but everything you said, it sounds like we can help you and the fact that you can't take your mom to chemo treatment every morning, that's terrible. So don't give up."

My point is you shouldn't have to convince them if you're following the relationship script and your screening questions and you're doing it correctly. It should be a natural path and progression and should be assumptive right to the next step for them to qualify, meaning having an appointment or whatever the call to action is. Or, if not qualifying, then you're going to have other services or resources that you're going to provide for them so that they can get help.

Wolfson: A lot of law firms ask us this question because they're confused. So when we talk about, "We're going to train your staff to convert more callers to cases," they say, "Well, isn't it a case or not and, quite simply, that's the job of the attorney." I want to reiterate what you're saying, Chris, which is not necessarily a matter of you're going to convince them or we're going to teach your staff to convince people to choose your law firm over another.

> **What you do have to keep in mind is that you are competing in a very competitive marketplace and your prospective clients have options.**

What you do have to keep in mind is that you are competing in a very competitive marketplace and your prospective clients have options. When they call your office, in many cases, it's not even a matter of persuasion or convincing. It's a matter of do you welcome that prospect with open arms and lead them down the path that they need to go on? Because they are an uninformed, uneducated buyer, meaning they don't know what they need, but they picked up the phone and called and they need someone who can help them.

Despite whatever they may say on the phone, in many cases they will try to control the call or they'll try and control the conversation. At the end of the day, they need expert help and assistance. And it's your intake staff's job to welcome every single one of those inquiry calls with open arms, and be eager and excited, and to realize that that's the source and the lifeblood of your business at a law firm.

Then take control of the call and follow a link, a sequential process, to uncover if this caller is qualified or not for your firm. Whether they are or they aren't, it doesn't mean they're going to love them any more or any less in terms of the relationship building. You have invested the money in marketing and advertising to generate the lead and to generate the inquiry.

How that call and inquiry is handled is just as important, if not more important, than all the resources that went into generating it from the outset. When we talk about saying, "Hey can we convince someone? Can we train your team to convert more callers to clients?" Not in the way that you're thinking about in terms of persuasion and convincing, but what we can do is give them a relationship building script.

We can give them the correct path to follow and we can give them a scorecard and a system so that they're held accountable so that they're doing it consistently. Because what you'll find is that many phone calls are good opportunities that simply get lost. They never make it into your "want" category. They never make it into the basket of, "Hey this is a qualified opportunity for us, for one reason or another." And that's a function of your intake team.

Mullins: The other thing I would add is that the word "convince" is not a good word because it lends itself to trickery. Most people who are not salespeople and have not had a career in sales look at that word as "ah hah, you're going to try to trick me." You're going to try trick these people into doing something they don't want to do because that's what salespeople do, they're so dishonest.

Wolfson: Maybe we should talk about some things like that. Let's talk about the word "convince," the word "persuasion" and let's talk about the word "sales" and how they relate to intake and a law firm.

Mullins: They're not good words because again they lend themselves to... most of the people we work with don't have a sales background so they will take those words as trickery and being dishonest and they will resist.

So what's better is teaching the team, which is what we do about sales. We teach them about relationships, communication and about how to do that using a tool which is called a script. We teach them as they follow the relationship-conversion-scripting principle — a natural outcome where the prospective client will agree to go to the next step, if they do it correctly.

Wolfson: I would think that we're saying, "Look, convincing someone to make a decision, or persuading them to make a decision, or influencing them to make a decision, in and of itself, is not a negative anything when it's done with integrity and when it's done with authenticity and honesty. For example, if someone picks up the phone, calls your office and they are in need and you believe in the professional service that you provide.

You have an obligation to walk them through the path and to go through your screening questions, to schedule an appointment, or to send an investigator, to try to help this person, to work with this person. And if we said you ultimately persuaded them or you convinced them to do that, okay, maybe you did, but as long as you do this with a principles-based approach, the words sales and convince and persuasion, in and of themselves, are not negative things.

But yes, it has a negative connotation and it's danced around when you think of law firms and the legal industry, meaning it's a professional industry, it's steeped in history and tradition and education.

So there are a lot of things with a negative connotation on the word sales. But again, if you want to be competitive in the market place, you have to do a better job of building those relationships with people when they call you. The other question that we get from the attorney is how do I tell my team we're going to record calls and monitor them without them getting mad and quitting or wanting to quit?

Mullins: First and foremost, you want to check the laws for recording phone calls in your state. I would not just off-the-cuff tell them, "Hey guys, this is what we're going to do and it's going to be okay so don't worry about it." That's not going to work. You need to sit down and script out the outline, the bullet points that you're going to share with them, prepared just like you would for a case.

And you first need to consider all their objections, just like in a typical conversation. They don't want their calls recorded, they don't want to hear their recorded voice, they don't want somebody listening to what they're saying. They're not interested in the big brother syndrome which is what they're going to think this is. Some of them are going to be thinking what you're doing is illegal and immoral.

Above all, they do not want to be held accountable for what they're saying. They don't want the rest of their team, let alone the attorney or the manager, to listen to the phone calls with them. Another objection they're going to have is that they're going to be held accountable, they have to critique their calls and their teammates are going to critique their calls. To prepare, write down the objections and put answers next to them. The answers would be, "Here's why we're going to do this. We're going to do this because we want to enhance what you're already doing right.

"We want to do this because it's an extremely competitive market. We're doing a great job, but we need to do better to stay in business and to stay ahead. We're spending a hundred to five hundred dollars every time a lead opts in, either by phone or by internet." Tell the team how much it is and that the firm needs to convert more of those leads. This is not about trying to catch people doing something wrong so we could fire them. This is not a setup, this is a brand new, ongoing coaching behavior modification program that will stay with us forever. It's not supposed to make anybody feel bad, tell them you're not going to give reviews and critiques by being mean or nasty. It's all going to be in the realm of training, coaching and feedback and helping and supporting each other because we're spending that monet just to get one prospect to call. Not to mention the competition and because we're afraid.

We want to stay ahead, we have to make sure that we inspect what we expect. We have to listen to the calls and how they're being handled so we can keep doing all the great things that we're doing because most of us don't even know what we're doing that's good because we just have a habit of going forward every day. We can fix the small areas so that we can convert more, that's what it's for. It's a positive motivation program, firm wide, for everybody.

Write down the objections and answer them in a way where you can coach them and roll it out in that format, make a big deal — a celebration — of it. "We have this program we're going to start. Here's what we're going to do." Put a system in place where you listen to recorded calls on a regular basis and let them know what that system is.

Tell them that they're not alone, that you're going to make sure they have ongoing coaching and support. We're not going to say, "Hey, this is the call you did for me, you did a lousy job." That's not what this is about. You want to unveil this as a new program that's going to help, not just beat the competition, not just give an incredible experience, but it's going to help team members to feel less stressful every single day. It's going to help the firm from the top-down, to put a spotlight on the team members to realize even more what an amazing thing that you do. That's why we're doing this.

Wolfson: What they need to do is share with their team, in a clear and meaningful way, the resources that are going into the leads and the phone calls, the marketing and advertising, meaning all the activity and resources that go into generating a call and break it down into a very clear, digestible number.

For example, we've done our research over the last year-and-a-half and looked at our marketing budget. It cost us $150 for every single inquiry call that comes in, period. Put $150 cash on the table and say, "That's what a phone calls looks like." Some people are going to be offended by that and some people are going to go, "Wow," and their eyes are going to open. "Wow, I didn't realize that."

What you would want to say is, something to the effect of, as a business owner, I have an obligation to put a commensurate investment of energy, time and resources into monitoring the accountability of our intake process and how we handle phone calls, meaning I'm holding my marketing accountable to one standard. I should be holding my intake process and lead conversion process to the same level of accountability to the best of my ability. Now it's nothing personal, it doesn't mean that you're a bad person, it doesn't mean that I'm trying to find you doing something wrong.

If anything, we look forward to identifying some of those gaps and those areas where we can course-correct, because people don't always know what to do and it doesn't mean that they're a bad person. So you shouldn't take this level of accountability personally. I also think that you should give people a grace period of, let's say, 30 days, maybe 60 days for them to feel uncomfortable and acknowledge the fact that they're going to feel uncomfortable. And say, "Okay, that's fine, that's part of this, it's part of getting used to it." Most people aren't comfortable with that, but at some level or another, they're ultimately going to have to be comfortable with it.

They also have to realize that everybody on the team is being held to the same standard. Ultimately the overriding principle is that people who are afraid of being held accountable for actual call recordings normally have a good reason to feel that way and they will self-select.

That may be a hard line, but at the end of the day, if you have somebody who's threatening to quit and they seem like, "Hey, this is a top performer and all of a sudden we're recording my calls," and they want to quit, I would have to scratch my head and question why is that, why do they feel that strongly about that. That they no longer want to perform now that you want to work in and pay attention to your business. You want to put a magnifying glass on the lifeblood of your business which is your telephone.

What I would say to that is look, if you look at any activity where you can measure it, measurement alone is what's going to help improve performance, and if you can't measure it then you can't manage it, whether it's athletics or needlepoint, I don't care what it is. If you want to be better, what you want to be able to do is go back and replay what happened, course-correct and identify, "Hey, you did these things really well. Or you did this and we could probably improve it." There's nothing wrong with saying that. The person who is uncomfortable taking that type of feedback most likely is not coachable.

> The person who is uncomfortable taking that type of feedback most likely is not coachable.

Obviously you would probably have a bigger problem than simply the call recording. Recording and monitoring your team at this level will simply bring to the surface those things that you may already know are there. So if you have this objection, is there something lingering that you have been avoiding? By putting this accountability in place, it brings to the surface those things that you've been avoiding and that's something you have to examine internally. But you shouldn't feel bad about saying, "I'm going to record my team and record my calls," because it's not personal. Chris, can't I just spend more money on marketing to get more clients?

Mullins: Yes, you can definitely do that and a lot of law firms do that, but it doesn't work. What's really happening is law firms are just ignoring the heavy lifting they need to do, the hard work. However long ago, they finally got the idea or embraced and accepted the whole concept of the word marketing. It was not something that law firms always understood, embraced or accepted.

But they got it and many law firms got connected with the right type of circles — mastermind circles and gurus — and learned the right types of marketing and basically got addicted to the whole of idea of spending money to get leads. Then they saw all those leads coming in, they spotted them as sales immediately and they got really excited about them.

But the big missing piece that is still quite simply beyond me is a lot of the firms that are doing very well. A lot of the firms might even be considered celebrity firms, and they're spending millions on marketing. They completely forgot about putting a step in place on what to do when that lead reaches out to you. They fell in love with the sexy concept of marketing and even competing with other firms.

Who's got the biggest marketing campaign? Who's got the biggest marketing program that seems to be successful because of all the leads coming in? The thinking just wasn't there and the dots were not connected. So no, if you spend more money on marketing, guess what's going to happen? You're going to get more leads, but that's not going to help you to convert the leads that you have.

What you have to do is focus on the whole process, not just on the leads that you get, but the leads that aren't being converted. How are they being converted, when are they being converted, are we even getting the right type of leads, is that marketing campaign even the right one for us, are we attracting the right types of clients? You can't just throw the money and see the leads come in and feel you're bigger and better, because that's just not the case.

So no, what you have to do is inspect what expect, find the right marketing program, and do an analysis if it is the right program, because not getting the right kinds of leads is whole other issue.

Make sure that you have a sales team in place, an inspection process in place, a coaching and training process in place to help your team. This would be for your attorneys, investigators, case managers, paralegals, intake specialists, receptionists, etc.

All of these people, giving the coaching they need so that they can handle the leads you have because you're bleeding, you're hemorrhaging. You're hemorrhaging because you have too many leads and you've got a team that you are paying to manage leads, period, not to convert, not to make them better, not to be successful.

Wolfson: I love it.

Mullins: Another question that comes up with the attorneys is, can I just spend more money on marketing to get more clients?

Wolfson: Yes, they can spend more money on marketing to get more clients, but it's very much like saying, "Can I pull more gas into the engine and am I going to get more out of it?" You will to some extent, but several things are going to happen in that case. You're acquisition cost is going to go up.

Basically you're saying it's going to cost you more and more money to generate those clients. You also may be attracting people who aren't necessarily qualified and you're going to tie up your operations. So the more money you spend on marketing and advertising just to throw more leads into the pot is ultimately going to lag your operations.

It's going to eat into your profitability versus if you take a really hard look at what are you're doing with the leads that you have, how many opportunities are you converting, what's being left on the table. Instead of putting more gas into the engine, to use that analogy, you start to figure out a way to be more efficient with what you have which is a much better way to invest your time, energy and resources than it is to simply spend more money on marketing.

Chris, you mentioned this point earlier that attorneys and law firms over the years have learned and they've mastered the game of marketing, to some extent, in terms of television advertising and this is in consumer law. We're talking personal injury, worker's comp, social security — all these areas where you can advertise on television. There's a call, a direct call to action, and you are trying to generate a lead.

So law firms have mastered that and it's a lot easier to simply write a check and spend money and say, "I'm going to throw more leads into my funnel and that's how we'll grow the business," than it is to develop your intake team and the people who are developing these relationships with callers and sorting through all the leads that come through the pipeline.

But if you start to focus on making that process more efficient, with a sales process with a principles-based training program, then you'll be even more effective. You can ultimately outspend your competitors in marketing and you can do it confidently that you're doing it profitably. The idea here is not, "Hey, we could just go out and spend more," but you can go and spend more profitably because you know your yield is higher.

This has everything to do with looking at how many leads you are currently leaving on the table, and from our experience, it is a significant number. This is even with the celebrity law firms, the million dollar spenders. They're spending big dollars on marketing and advertising and they're leaving gobs and gobs of opportunities on the table. Now here's what this does. Ultimately it creates ill will in the marketplace. You can ride on your brand and you can ride on the strength of your resources for a long time. But at some point or another, you will develop a reputation in the marketplace as a churn-and-burn operation, meaning you're churning and burning through leads. And that's okay if you can live with that reputation.

Even those firms who may have developed that reputation over a period of time, because of the amount of marketing and advertising that they're doing in their internal processes, can recover from that and do even better simply by focusing on intake.

Mullins: The other thing I'll just throw in is you're stressing out your team. You're spending all this money to get more leads to come, which means the phones are ringing off the hook, and you haven't increased your staff, even temporary staff, to adapt to the periodic campaigns that you do. In fact, you're not even telling your staff that you're going to do these campaigns, and they should get ready because the potential amount of calls coming through.

You should have a backup team where you can call in the troops to help out, even a temporary team when you have those big campaigns. But what you're doing is stressing out your team, abusing your team because you're not even telling them, you're throwing all this volume to them. They have to process this volume, which is not generating anything except calls for everybody.

You're losing your team, you're losing their respect, and you're also losing them because the front desk, the receptionist, the intake person, the call center, the folks that handle those kinds of positions, it's a revolving door and you have to constantly replace those positions. They can't handle it if the burnout is massive. You don't have any relationship currency, if you will, with your own internal team which are your internal clients.

Wolfson: So it's almost a new day for the legal industry to start to become masters of the intake part, the sales part, the relationship building part, the conversion side of the business. We've done a good job on the marketing, meaning we're there, we have arrived. But to focus all of our energy and effort and to still constantly look at the latest and greatest shiny object, whether it's internet marketing or television advertising or whatever it is, to generate leads is not the best area that you can focus. The best area that you can focus on is conversion and it's a new day in that regard.

Mullins: Yep, it's a new day.

Wolfson: How do I record calls and what are the recording laws I need to be aware of?

Mullins: There are a few different ways you can record phone calls, and that's a good question about recording laws. It is your responsibility to check online with your state to find out what the most recent recording laws are. Ignorance is not an excuse, you need to do that and pay attention to it. Once you figure out what the laws are, if it's okay for you to record, this is a very easy, extremely inexpensive, low risk system — automated and web-based.

> It's a new day.

And there's no long-term contract. In most cases, you can cancel with a 30-day notice if for some reason you don't want to do it anymore. But it's pretty simple. You find a provider... and we provide this service in Intake Academy because it's part of scoring calls for your staff. There's no equipment necessary or anything, you get a call tracking phone number, it's a special phone number, maybe a local number to your area.

That local phone number gets published in one of your marketing campaigns — maybe you would put it on your billboards, commercials, your website. So you chose your billboard, you have it published on there and don't worry because everything's going to be okay. When the prospect sees that billboard and your message speaks to them, they're going to call that number.

And because they called that number, it's going to be forwarded to your office. Nothing's going to be different for the prospect calling you, they're going to get your office just like you want them to. When it rings at your office, nothing's going to be different for the receptionist or the intake team that's handling the call. They're going to get the same call that they always do.

But the big secret and the big difference is because the prospective clients who call that tracking number, all the phone calls that go to that number are immediately recorded, tracked, monitored and scored online. What that means for you as a business owner is that you'll be able to measure your return of investment on marketing dollars immediately. You'd go online, type in the password, click on your tracking number and boom! You're going to see every single phone call that went into that call tracking number for that billboard campaign. You're going to be able to easily say, "Wow! Look at all those calls I got." Or you'll say, "Oh my God, I'm getting no calls."

Maybe you're going to change the campaign, but when you're getting the calls, you're going to be excited, you're going to know that you're doing the right thing. But more importantly, and this is where the Intake Academy comes in, every phone call is recorded. You can easily click on a call and hear the conversation. And that's magical because not only can you hear it, not only can your supervisor hear it, not only can your team hear it, but the Intake Academy can listen to the call and score it to train and teach your team. It's really easy.

Wolfson: This is great.

Mullins: Yes, this is excellent. But let's continue this conversation in Volume II.

Wolfson: Okay, sounds good.

Mullins: Thanks, bye.

Resource: To get more of Chris Mullins and her **FREE Monday Morning Email Stimulators**™, opt in at www.GreatBottomLine.com.
   Don't forget to call (603) 924-1640 on how to join our **Monday Morning Role Play Hot Seat**.

Chapter Five

Intake Academy Newsletter

An Interview From the Intake Academy Newsletter

Are you on our newsletter mailing list? Read this interview where Chris Mullins interviews Micki Love, COO of Hughes & Coleman, in one of the Intake Academy newsletter's expert interview series. If you're not receiving the Intake Academy newsletter and would like to, please email beth@intakeacademy.com and ask her to put you on our mailing list. Each month you'll get articles and interviews from people in the industry — your industry. See how they're dealing with the same challenges as your office and how the Intake Academy can help.

Love: Hi, Chris. It's Micki. How are you?

Mullins: I'm super, Micki. How are you? Are you excited?

Love: I am. I'm very excited. Nothing better than intake topics, right?

Mullins: Right. We're just going to dive right in. It's going to be very informal; just two gals hanging out, chit-chatting, okay?

Love: Fantastic!

Mullins: That's really the way to look at it. I told you and I emailed you that I wanted to interview you for the expert interview series because, truthfully, when I met you, I just felt that you were probably like the diamond in the bunch, right?

Love: Well, thank you.

Mullins: I mean, I've run businesses for years and it's not easy to have great people. To me, you don't have a job, you have a passion.

Love: I've grown up with it and it's something that I love — the job of helping people. My job really is helping the staff we have here to continue to have jobs for a long time, and part of that is instilling in them the core values that the partners had when they built this firm. Sometimes it's hard to continue those traditions and bring those cultures to life, but I do have a passion for making sure they know what drove Marshall and Lee (M&L) to want to do this business.

Mullins: Take me back to the beginning. How long have you been doing this? Give me a little snapshot of what happened and how you got where you are right now.

Love: Oh, my goodness. I started with the firm in 1993 as a runner and file clerk while I was attending college, and very quickly decided that I was going to do college courses at night and work during the day. So I became a receptionist, which is where I really got introduced into the importance of the new call. Mr. Hughes was very adamant that every new caller was to be taken care of from the moment they called in. They needed to be made to feel like they called the right place.

He would test me every day. He would call and he would be that new client or that new caller just to make sure I was on top of my game. He taught me about having a mirror in front of you when you're on the phone with a client.

Mullins: Oh, wow.

Love: Because it helps bring that spirit out so that you smile when you're on the phone. It translates through the phone. He was really the passionate one about the phone call and making sure we tracked everything and knew where the client heard about us, knew their name and treated them with respect. That's how I got passionate about intake and new clients and the business aspect of bringing the calls into the firm.

From there, I moved into the accounting department — I have an accounting degree. I was there for a while, but my passion really drove me to the business side of it and I wanted to learn more about how to make the phones ring and how to make more business for the partners. I moved into the marketing department, and with marketing comes the intake process because it all ties together.

I continued to learn every job there was in the building because I figured if I knew more about what each person's position was, then I would have a better idea of what the clients needed to hear on the front end and what they needed from us in the form of advertising so that we could continue to build our brand, deliver excellent customer service and continue to grow the firm.

Mullins: How long ago was this?

Love: I started in 1993 and spent two years as a receptionist and probably two years in accounting. The rest of my tenure here at the firm has been marketing and management.

Mullins: Mr. Hughes was on top of and concerned about all the details of the client or the prospect on the phone? That's amazing.

Love: Oh, absolutely. Back then, at the front desk, we had a printed Excel spreadsheet. We didn't even keep it in the computer because it was old DOS versions of Windows back then. We had a piece of paper we printed out every day and we would start over and write down the client's name and the source they heard about us from.

At the end of the day, we had to tally all that up and send it to him with a report of, "We had this many calls today. This many came from this source. These two were referred by this person, and this happened with this other client. Here's the outcome of what happened with those clients today. We signed up four, we disengaged three and two of them we're chasing. We're sending these letters as a referral source, thank-you letters, etc." So we had a whole slew of what we now use software to do. We were doing it all manually back in 1993.

Mullins: I just think it's amazing, because I've been in this business for 30 years now coaching, consulting and teaching law firms how to improve conversion via the telephone and I still find that with clients, even in 2014, there's a big struggle with understanding what you just laid out that Mr. Hughes was so passionate about in 1993. I think it's really great, and they're fortunate and you're fortunate that you've been part of that whole picture from the early days. That's awesome!

Love: I was very fortunate to have some great leaders and very open-minded individuals who were willing to look. "What is it? What do we need to know in order to get better and to be able to absorb that information?" Of course, being part of M&L, I get to sit in the same room with a bunch of great advertising and business-minded men twice a year and listen to them throw out ideas. My challenge is to find the ideas that sound really great, bring them back and try to implement them to make our firm even better. So I've been very fortunate and blessed to have been placed in that situation over and over again.

Mullins: Yes, and I want to make sure that everyone reading this interview all know that this interview is based on fast-forward right now. Back in 1993, and even in 2000, I imagine it wasn't always easy. It's not easy now, but I don't want law firms that read this to say, "Oh. Well, that's Hughes & Coleman, and that's M&L, and they're way up there." I want people to realize that they can be exactly where you are, no matter where they are right now, that it's reachable.

Love: Absolutely. When I started, we were one law firm, one location, with a sheet of paper and all it took was business partners who were dedicated to growing, open-minded individuals like myself and others who were willing to look for that information that the business-minded partners were saying we needed to know in order to grow, and then applying what you were learning as you went every day.

We've made a ton of mistakes. We've advertised in places that you should never advertise, we've answered the phones and done things with new calls that you would never want to do, but out of every experience we've learned something, and we've revamped our process and figured out, "Okay, that didn't work, but if we do X, Y and Z instead, we can do a better job for the clients or we can get more clients," or whatever the process is that we're working on at the moment.

The challenge is not to be afraid to make a mistake, because you're going to, and as long as you're making mistakes, then you're growing in some way. You'll learn something and you're going to get better. As long as you're willing to learn from it and grow, then you can only go up.

Mullins: Right. That's important. What I find by communicating with my clients is that with the Intake Academy, there are definitely clients who don't want to rock the boat with their team by getting involved with, let's say, tracking every detail of the call or recording calls and playing them back, or critiquing and monitoring calls, or holding people accountable for using a script. Whatever the new change is, there are a lot of firms that don't want to upset the existing team.

Love: I have a couple of comments on that. I think the first one is that people respect what you inspect and expect out of them, so if you expect them to help you grow your firm, then they're going to respect that and want to help you achieve that goal.

For me, it was always about putting the goal out there, letting the staff know, "Hey, what if we did this this month?" and then setting a reward for that goal with, "Let's go get it!" and igniting our staff to want to be our passionate disciples, telling people about you, wanting to get you where you want to be. They've got to believe in you in order to believe in the process and in order to believe that by you getting better, their lives are also going to get better. Make sure they can see your vision and then reward them when you get there, or along the way. I think that keeps them ignited and excited, and eventually they're going to learn what is important to you.

We're very open at our firm. We tell the staff all the numbers, whatever it is that we're working toward. Give them the goal. Most people are very good at figuring out how to help you achieve that goal. If you set a goal for them and they know that it's important to you, they're going to want to help you as long as they can see the passion in you about where the firm is going. As long as you don't show hesitancy and you show them where you're trying to go, they're going to go with you.

Mullins: How do you get it all done? Remember, you're speaking to all kinds of law firms. What do you say to those folks who want to stick their toes in but, for lack of a better word, are afraid? Like maybe it's better to look the other way.

Love: Let's baby-step it. Pick out one goal that you want to achieve — a short-term goal — for one quarter. Set that goal. If that goal is to increase referrals by 10 percent, tell them what that 10 percent equates to. If it's 15, if it's five, if it's three referrals for the quarter, set it out there and then have a brief meeting with the staff. "If we achieve this, then we're going to have a pizza party." But first you have to know what it is you want to achieve.

I think it comes from the top. The top person has to know, "Where do I want to go and how am I going to get there?" Start by getting your staff engaged and excited about getting to that big-picture vision, because it's really hard for non-business-minded individuals to absorb the whole picture at one time. They need bite-sized pieces they can consume and get behind and get engaged with and then help you grow toward that big picture. Figure out what you want and go get it.

Mullins: I would add to that to begin with something. But before you go ahead and decide on what that one baby step is going to be, make darn sure that you are going to hold yourself accountable for following through with it — period.

In other words, you don't want to just go ahead and make the announcement, "We're going to focus on this goal this month" and then not pay attention, not communicate about it and have it fall through the cracks. Make sure you pick a goal that you really believe that you can hold yourself accountable to, right?

Love: Absolutely, and if the person at the top cannot be the one to hold people accountable and to put the numbers out there and to give the praise, then assign the project to someone on your team who's really good at those things and let them go with it. It can be an empowering moment for that person who's good at encouragement and leadership. Let them be the one who gives out the reports and sings the praises. The rest of the staff just have to know that the person at the top is backing them and supporting them in accomplishing this. And let it go. It'll work.

Mullins: Just dive in and do it. And not everything is supposed to be perfect. You're going to learn from it.

Love: Absolutely.

Mullins: What about your intake team right now? What is the big focus with them that you're trying to help and support them with when it comes to conversion?

Love: Educating them. We are trying every day to make sure that they understand what it is that we're looking for and why we are looking for it so they're not just going through the motions. They need to understand how they, as an individual taking a phone call, are helping someone on the other end of the line. We've used Intake Academy for a while. We put a lot of techniques into place that you've taught us. We do daily huddles and we're starting to see dramatic changes in the intake staff's perception of their role in the firm.

I don't want them to come in everyday just thinking, "Oh, I've just got to sit here and answer this phone." That's not it at all. They are the lifeline to tomorrow for us, so make sure they understand that and make sure they understand that they are somebody's hero today or that they've been a rock for somebody who has really broken down. They're our bridge to get from point A to point B with this law firm. They need to feel appreciated and respected.

When I ask the question, "What can we do to show you we appreciate you," it isn't about money. Of course, they all like to be paid more, but that isn't the thing that comes up. Over and over it's, "We want to understand more about what types of cases the firm wants and why they want them. What are they going to do with them when they get them?" I think that educating them is empowering to these individuals and so it helps them help us be a better firm.

Mullins: You folks are doing a great job at it, and working with the Intake Academy obviously is a great springboard into that. I think it's important for everybody to make sure that, at the end of the day, they're catching somebody doing something right in the firm. Not just intake, but having the habit and behavior of catching someone doing something right everyday.

I think that you're doing great. You're on the right path, especially the hero path, because as long as the team, from the top down, knows the real purpose for what they're doing, the human part of what they're doing with every prospect and client, if they're reminded of that, whether it's through a scorecard or listening to a call or sitting down in a huddle talking about prospective clients that have the potential of becoming clients. As long as everybody realizes the real human part of what they do, I think the sky's the limit.

Love: I agree. I think it all starts with your team, and so you keep them engaged and excited and the sky's the limit, just like you said.

Mullins: One question I have for you is how the heck do you do it all? I mean, you have a family, right?

Love: I have a really great team that I work with and a lot of support here at the office. We don't have a lot of management support. I don't mean that in the manner of I just have extra people laying around all the time, but I have a lot of people who feel empowered in their jobs and who are passionate about the firm just like I am, and so it helps to make sure that we get through the day.

I think that the hardest thing sometimes is remembering to stop and give thanks to those who are helping us to get where we're trying to be and to find that one praise a day and to hand it out in a sincere manner, not just in an email and not just, "Hey, good job!" I really want to try and deliver those things on an ongoing basis that help them to know that we know that their job is not easy and we appreciate the effort and the energy they're putting into it.

Those inner connections that you make with the staff, letting them know how you feel about them, that's the hardest part to find the time to do, so it's my daily devotion to myself to make sure I get out there and do that.

Mullins: I'll give a suggestion on a way to help do that, and I call it "relationship currency." It's a good question for everybody to ask themselves in their business. "Do you have relationship currency with your team when you really think about it?"

Most people can answer that question pretty quickly, but what you can do is take your calendar this very moment and schedule a recurring event. Call it "relationships," call it "relationship currency," call it "love taps" — whatever you want to call it. Schedule it every day, whether it's five, 10 or 15 minutes for the rest of the year, so it pops up and is a reminder to you.

Love: One of the love taps that we do, Chris, that the staff seems to enjoy a lot is a letter to their family at home just letting the family know how much we appreciate them sharing their mom or their dad or their sister or whomever with us. We know that it's not easy to have their parents committed to a full-time job or being away from the home many hours throughout the day. We appreciate that they spend the time with us and we try to include some passage that their clients have said about their parent or loved one, or that a co-worker has said, and that seems to go really far in the community and with the co-workers here as well.

Mullins: I want to make sure I got this right. Did you say that what Hughes & Coleman does is send thank-yous to the families for allowing their mom or dad or whomever to be with you and work with you and work so hard?

Love: Yes.

Mullins: That's really awesome. That's really cool. What is it that you send them? How do you do that?

Love: I do a personalized letter. It takes two or three minutes to hand-write one and send it out thanking them for the day. And I'll find some quotes. Usually I'll get feedback throughout the day of, "This client said this great thing about staff X," or a co-worker will pass me in the hall and say, "You know what? So-and-so really helped me do this today and I think it would really make a difference."

At the end of the day, when I'm wrapping up and I'm ready to do love taps, I sit down and jot a letter to X client or X employee's family members and include those little quotes I learned about them throughout the day, how they made a difference in the life of someone and how appreciative I am.

Mullins: That's really great. Well, everybody has a team at the office and you have a team at home, too. I imagine your team at home is very supportive for you to be such a successful businesswoman running Hughes & Coleman, right?

Love: I hope so.

Mullins: So you get kudos!

Love: It takes a village.

Mullins: It really does. Well, I think everything that you folks are doing is great, keep doing it. M&L Group is a terrific group. Obviously, it's your way of being able to give back to so many firms to keep it going, to keep the chain going of firms that believe in internal customer service first, and when you give to the internal team, you win so much more from your external clients and prospective clients.

Love: I would agree.

Mullins: Any last words you want to say to anybody? Any words of wisdom or hope?

Love: No, I'm just very thankful to have had this opportunity to share any little bit of information that I have with everyone, and I'm always willing to share more. Anybody can reach out to me anytime. I'm here and available.

I did want to tell you, Chris, that we've done a new video about one of our bridge-building activities with our intake staff, so I'm going to be sending you a clip of that here in just a little bit. You can have that for your video library.

Mullins: So what is the video?

Love: We do the intake huddles twice a week and we have challenges. This video is the bridge-building challenge, and the lesson for the intake huddle was how they are the bridge between the client's first impression of the firm in the sign-up.

Mullins: Beautiful. Wow.

Love: They had to build a bridge without speaking with their teammates and show how difficult it can be for them to really understand all the processes that are involved when they don't understand the terminology and all the steps necessary to make something happen. We did a little exercise and a video to go with it. It's fun and we're going to share it with you just to thank you for helping us come up with some ideas to motivate and inspire our intake team.

Mullins: That is so awesome. I can't tell you... you just made my day. That is so great. I am so happy. I'm a teacher, consultant, coach and trainer, so when I hear feedback, not just numbers on conversions, but actual feedback, changes that are being made even if they're just baby steps, it's music to my ears. I really appreciate you saying that. I can't wait to see the video.

Love: We'll get it over to you this afternoon.

Mullins: All right. Well, take it easy. Thank you so much for your time. It was great speaking with you, Micki, and everybody's going to learn a lot by reading this.

Love: I appreciate that, Chris. You have a great day.

Mullins: Thank you. Bye now.

Chris Mullins Quiet Rooms for Law Firms™
Training for the Brain

First, we have to acknowledge where $300 billion in healthcare costs is going. Healthcare costs to businesses skyrocket when employees don't feel well. There are five aspects to health — mental, emotional, physical, social and spiritual. We give our employees a comfortable, safe place to work, and often a gym to exercise in... that's physical. We are opening up the work environment to create spaces to collaborate... that's social. Spiritual is really not in the realm of companies to address so what are we doing about emotional and mental health? Especially when you think of the types of phone calls, prospects and clients your teams' firm deal with every single day.

We're working our employees to the burnout point. We expect them to produce, produce, produce. And we want them to be "on" 24/7. That does not promote mental and emotional well-being. That is not how to grow your business and it's not how you will keep insurance costs down, as well as the huge cost of constantly hiring new people.

Chris Mullins Quiet Rooms for Law Firms™ — call (603) 924-1640 or email beth@intakeacademy.com or chris@mullinsmediagroup.com.

How Does Your Firm Have Fun and Show Appreciation to Your Super Heroes?

Here's how one firm is having fun and motivating their team with the super hero program.

The team at The Sawaya Law Firm went all out with this terrific giant superhero poster and took pictures of the whole team like these (with Attorney Mike Sawaya to the right).

What can your firm do to take a break and have some fun while showing how much you appreciate your team? Be creative and send us your pictures!

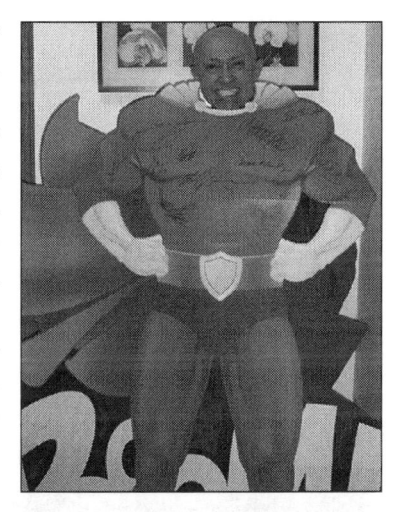

Intake Academy Services

Would you like your own call center? We build call centers for you! Call (603) 924-1640 to learn more about this service.

Add These Events Below to Your Calendar...

To register, call (603) 924-1640, email beth@intakeacademy.com or chris@mullinsmediagroup.com.

- International Intake Sales Specialist Week™ – September
- Legal Intake Specialist Association™ (LISA) – Boot Camp – October
- Legal Intake Specialist 911™ – a 911 support hotline for Intake Specialists to call and get LIVE support to vent with no repercussions after handling a difficult phone call. Questions? Call (603) 924-1640.

Intake Academy Members and Clients Will Receive Customized Sales Coaching, Consulting and Training for...

- How to Hire Intake Sales Managers
- Inbound and Outbound Phone Sales
- Case Managers – *customer service, empathy, relationship, communication, retention and sales*
- Attorney – *empathy, scripts, sales, relationship, communication and retention*
- Intake Specialists   ➤ Call Center   ➤ Legal Assistants
- First Impressions Director, Receptionist
- Monthly Coaching With Intake Academy Heroes and Our In-House Certified Coaches
- Monthly Q&A Attorney-Only Mastermind Conference Calls
- Monthly Q&A Staff-Only Mastermind Conference Calls
- Monthly Q&A How to Hire Intake Sales Heroes Conference Calls
- Weekly Monday Morning Role Play Hot Seat
- Intake Academy Gold Standard Conversion Script
- Gold Standard Certification
- Team First Certification

INTAKE™ ACADEMYLLC
www.IntakeAcademy.com
A Division of Mullins Media Group™ LLC
(603) 924-1640

Attorneys Only
Get Your FREE Mystery Call and Conversion Debrief
Go to **www.IntakeAcademy.com** and on the first page just click on *Sign Up for Free Mystery Call*. As you go through the sign-up, don't forget to schedule your **Attorney-Only** and **Chris Mullins Mystery Call Conversion Debrief**.

We're Growing!

And We're Looking for Phone Coaches and Trainers

The Intake Academy™ LLC is looking for speakers, actors, teachers, trainers or salespeople to be Intake Phone Coaches for law firms. The Intake Academy provides training and coaching to consumer law firms throughout North America. We help improve staff performance at the critical point of contact — when prospective clients call the law firm for the first time to inquire about a potential case. How inquiry calls are handled during the intake process has a dramatic impact on the success of a firm, and can be improved through on-going training, coaching and reinforcement.

The Intake Academy is looking for a phone coach who will provide monthly coaching and training for our clients. This project requires:

- Individuals that, above all else, regardless of the project, job, assignment or task they've been given to do, their main focus both personally and professionally is to always make absolutely sure it is done exceptionally well and with the utmost integrity, no matter what curve balls have been thrown.
- Exceptional telephone and sales communication skills
- Facilitation, coaching and presenting skills
- A strong desire and passion for teaching, personal and professional development
- The ability to objectively listen to phone calls and provide meaningful coaching and feedback
- The ability to master and follow the Intake Academy training and coaching process to achieve results
- Punctual scheduling and exceptional time management skills
- Willingness to learn, grow, pay great attention to detail and who can follow directions

Project Description

This project consists of preparing and hosting private and group telephone coaching sessions via telephone conference call with legal intake staff, receptionists, paralegals and attorneys from various law firms throughout North America. Prior to hosting coaching calls, the coach must review recorded intake phone calls, prepare coaching points in advance and score intake calls using the Intake Academy™ coaching system. Building and maintaining client relationships is critical for a coach. During the coaching call, your specific focus is to help the team members identify what worked well, what the areas of opportunity are and specifically what they can do to improve or fix problem areas. All of the coaching is focused exclusively on the legal intake process. Prior to starting the coaching project, you must become certified by the Intake Academy, which requires a minimum of 45 days. Candidates will complete background checks and assessments.

This is a tremendous opportunity for the right person looking for a flexible, virtual project delivered from your home office, who has a strong desire to help coach, train and develop legal intake staff. At the Intake Academy, we know the front desk staff (receptionists, intake specialist, paralegals and intake attorneys) are often the unsung heroes of the law firm.

Intake is the lifeblood for our clients, but most law firms are so focused on marketing and practicing law that they lose sight of how critically important intake truly is to their business, and in many cases the frontline staff are overworked, underappreciated and don't have the training and ongoing feedback they need to be successful. This — appreciation, coaching, training, feedback, systems — is what we provide to our clients, and that is what this project is all about. To apply, please follow these instructions...

- Email beth@intakeacademy.com your updated resumé as a Word document attachment. Include your complete updated contact information, email, phone and address.

- Include with your resumé, three business work references to include complete contact information, phone and email, name of business and mailing address for all three references.

- a) Include in the same email, as a Word document attachment, what was it, specifically, that you read about this opportunity that made you decide to submit your information? b) Why, specifically, are you looking for projects and work?

- Candidates that complete all of the above instructions will be contacted via email for the next step.